IMAGES
of America

BREWING IN CLEVELAND

P.O.C. Beer is one of the most fondly remembered brands of beer ever made in Cleveland. The brand first appeared prior to 1910 and continued to be brewed at the west side plant of the Pilsener Brewing Company until its closing in 1962. The brand was then made in Pittsburgh until 1972, after which its production returned to Cleveland until 1984. This advertising sign is from the 1940s and connects the brand to one of the city's favorite participation sports: bowling.

IMAGES
of America

BREWING IN CLEVELAND

Robert A. Musson, M.D.

ARCADIA
PUBLISHING

Published by Arcadia Publishing
Charleston, South Carolina

Library of Congress Catalog Card Number: 2005933419

For all general information contact Arcadia Publishing at:
Telephone 843-853-2070
Fax 843-853-0044
E-mail sales@arcadiapublishing.com
For customer service and orders:
Toll-Free 1-888-313-2665

Visit us on the Internet at www.arcadiapublishing.com

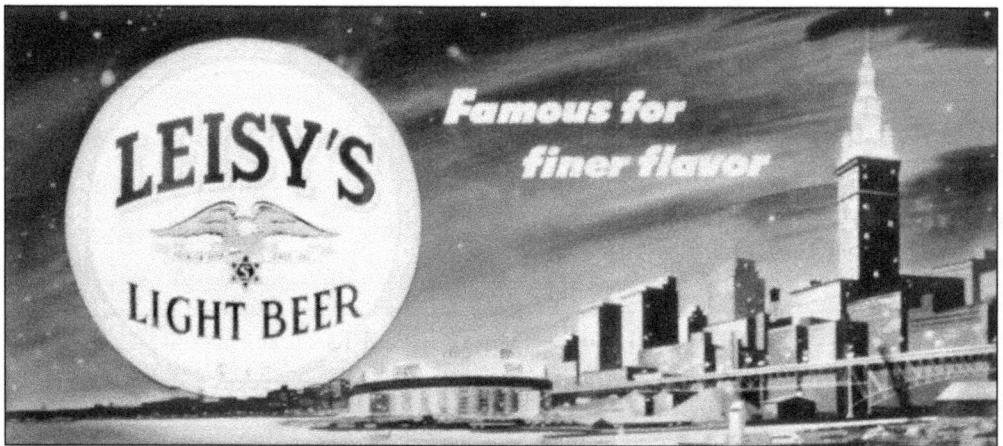

Leisy Beer is another fondly remembered brand from Cleveland. Made at the west side plant of the Leisy Brewing Company until 1959, the brand name was always associated with top-quality beer. The company was operated by Leisy family members throughout its existence. A few buildings and the smokestack from the brewery complex still remain visible from Interstate 90, just west of downtown. This is a sign from the early 1950s showing the city's skyline from Lake Erie. (Bill Carlisle collection.)

CONTENTS

ACKNOWLEDGMENTS

No book project is ever completed without the assistance and support of others. I want to thank my wife and best friend, Jenny, who has been supportive of this and my other book projects throughout our marriage. I would like to dedicate the book to our daughter Anastasia Marie, who should be born by the time the book is published.

In addition, I would like to thank Carl Miller, who helped me get my start in writing about the history of the brewing industry and has lent me many images from his personal collection for this and my other books. Along those lines, I would also like to thank Bill Carlisle and Don Augenstein for lending me many images from their collections for this project. Others have lent their assistance with images as well and are listed throughout the book. I would also like to thank my editor, Melissa Basilone, for assistance and support. Arcadia has made the creation of this project extraordinarily easy, compared with the self-publication of my previous writing endeavors.

For additional information on the subject of Cleveland breweries, I highly recommend the following books:

Miller, Carl. *Breweries of Cleveland*. Cleveland: Schnitzelbank Press, 1998.

Musson, Robert A., M.D. *Brewing Beer in the Buckeye State, Volume I*. Medina, Ohio: Zepp Publications, 2005.

One Hundred Years of Brewing. Chicago and New York: H. S. Rich and Company, 1903.

Van Wieren, Dale P. *American Breweries II*. West Point, PA: Eastern Coast Breweriana Association, 1995.

INTRODUCTION

The brewing of beer, like other spirits, is well documented as having begun in the earliest days of recorded civilizations, thousands of years ago, although brewing in some form was likely taking place even earlier than that. Beer in various forms (or similar beverages) was popular in nearly every culture, not only for its inebriating effects but also because of the nature of its production, which involved the boiling of ingredients prior to fermentation, during which alcohol was created. The combination assured that all potentially harmful bacteria were killed off, making the brew safe for drinking while the water sources in many areas were not known to be pure. This was especially true for explorers and settlers in new lands, where local water quality was often questionable.

While the first commercial brewery in the New World is generally accepted to have been in New Amsterdam in 1612, Ohio's first brewery is the subject of some debate. Surely many domestic home-brewing operations existed among the earliest settlers, but the state's first commercial brewer of any significance remains unclear. Depending on the source of the information, however, it is generally accepted that the first one was within five years of Ohio's statehood in 1803, either in Cincinnati or Zanesville. According to *One Hundred Years of Brewing*, the state had 13 brewers by 1809–1810, but the size and extent of these early enterprises, not to mention their exact locations, remains a mystery.

The products of these earliest breweries were generally varieties of beer, ale, porter, and stout, as these were the typical malt beverages of the English-speaking culture that settled Ohio. The word "beer" is actually a generic term that can refer to a wide variety of beverages made from the fermentation of the extract of malted grain. The grain used for malting is most commonly barley, but others, such as corn, rice, and wheat, can be used as well.

The city of Cleveland was a relatively late bloomer with regard to the brewing industry. Founded in 1796 by Gen. Moses Cleaveland, a surveyor for the Connecticut Land Company, the city initially began as a settlement near the mouth of the Cuyahoga River, at its junction with Lake Erie. Further development took the town out of the river valley and up to a flat plain just to the east, where the current public square exists today. After its founding, it was still more than 30 years later before the town began to grow rapidly, due to the completion in 1832 of the Ohio and Erie Canal, a 308-mile transportation link between the Great Lakes and the Ohio River. Paralleling the Cuyahoga River at its origin, the canal began in Cleveland's Flats section, making the city a key geographic and economic site for the Great Lakes region.

Not surprisingly, the city's first brewery appeared in the year that the canal was completed, and numerous others soon followed. Most of the early brewers opened for business in the Flats area and were primarily ale brewers, but as time went by and the city began to grow away from the Flats, more of the brewers began to spread out as well. Ale was a popular beverage in the city's early years, although once German immigrants began to settle in Cleveland, bringing their newly discovered and highly popular lager beer with them, enthusiasm for ale slowly eroded until the end of the 19th century, by which time nearly all of the city's ale brewers had either closed or converted their plants to the production of lager beer.

A huge influx of German immigrants arrived in Cleveland between the 1840s and the 1880s, bringing much of their culture with them. The particular process for the production of lager beer was one aspect, and it would revolutionize the American beer industry within a fairly short time. The first lager beer in America is thought to have been brewed around 1840, and it is believed that it was first brewed in Cleveland in either the late 1840s or the early 1850s. Despite its taking longer to produce (key factors in the production of lager beer are its need to be produced at colder temperatures than ale and its need to be stored for weeks or months before serving), the flavor of lager made it far more popular in the long run, and virtually all of the brewers who thrived in the late 19th century did so because of their production of lager beer.

As the industry continued to develop, huge breweries were constructed throughout the city, mostly carrying German names such as Schlather, Gehring, Leisy, Beltz, and Diebolt. By the 1890s, however, the economics of the brewing industry caused a great deal of competition between rival brewers, leading to the formation of a huge combine known as the Cleveland and Sandusky Brewing Company. Eventually encompassing 14 breweries in three cities, the combine dominated beer sales in the region up until the beginning of Prohibition in 1919.

During the Prohibition era, many of the companies that had flourished previously were either shut down completely or their business was cut back severely, despite their attempts to find other ways to utilize their facilities, either via soft drink and ice production or even coal distribution. Some stayed in business purely through management of their real estate properties. Nevertheless, those that returned to brewing after the repeal of Prohibition in 1933 found the landscape of the industry to be very different than in the past.

After Prohibition's end, 10 companies began to brew beer, and most found success in the 1930s and 1940s. However, after World War II, advances in technology and transportation allowed larger national brewers to compete with the local companies, and in the 1950s, most were unable to keep up; between 1952 and 1962, five of the largest breweries in the city closed or were sold. By 1972, only one remained in the city, and it closed its doors in 1984, bringing the era of big brewers in Cleveland to an end.

Beginning in 1988, the city saw a rebirth of the industry on a smaller scale, as numerous brewpubs and several microbreweries appeared throughout the region, bringing high-quality craft beers to a welcome public. Craft beers took on an almost unlimited number of styles and tastes, with each brewer bringing his own artistic vision of what a beer or ale should taste like, and many of them took one back to what some of the earliest English ales and German lagers might have tasted like more than a century earlier. In this sense, the industry has nearly come full circle, bringing us to the publication of this book in 2005. It is hoped that readers take some of the city's brewing history into consideration if they happen to enjoy a Cleveland-made brew in the future. Cheers!

One

THE ORIGINS OF A
LOCAL INDUSTRY
1830s–1890s

The Cleveland Brewery was the city's first such establishment when it opened in 1832. Located in the Flats district, along the Ohio and Erie Canal, the brewery was founded by Robert Bennett and local physician Dr. Samuel J. Weldon. After changing ownership several times, the plant was rebuilt in 1847 and purchased by Samuel C. Ives. The drawing above appeared in the *Cleveland Plain Dealer* in 1863 and shows a larger addition from 1852, shown on the right side. The plant continued to operate until 1865, when a Confederate sympathizer set the buildings on fire near the end of the Civil War, and the plant burned to the ground.

KINDSVATER & MALL BREWERY. CLEVELAND, O.

Lith. by A. Tailleudar & Co. 219 Superior St. Cleveland, O.

The Lion Brewery had its origins in 1850 when it was founded by Martin Stumpf, the city's first brewer of lager beer, although he sold the brewery in 1859 to Jacob Mall and Paul Kindsvater. Located atop a steep bluff overlooking Lake Erie, it would remain in operation until 1944. This image is a lithograph from the late 1860s, showing the brewery with sailboats on the lake in the background. (Bob and Jeanette Bendula collection, courtesy of Carl Miller.)

AUGUST BURCKHARDTS BREWERY COR. OF PEARL & MONROE STS. CLEVELAND OHIO

August Burckhardt founded a small lager beer brewery in 1868 along Pearl Street (later West Twenty-fifth Street), on the city's near west side. Producing around 2,500 barrels of beer annually, it was sold in 1876 to Anton Kopp, and after two more changes of ownership, the plant closed its doors in 1880. This drawing appeared in the *Cleveland City Atlas of 1874*.

Carl Ernst Gehring was born in 1830 in Goeppingen, Wurttemberg, Germany. After coming to America at age 18, he worked in several different breweries, including that of John M. Hughes, where he developed a reputation as a respected brewmaster before founding his own plant on the city's near west side in 1857. Although he had brewed ale in his previous jobs, he found much greater success on his own with the brewing of lager beer.

This is Carl Gehring's original brewery, as drawn for the *Cleveland City Atlas of 1874*. At the time, it had a 155-barrel brew kettle, which was the largest in the city, allowing it to produce around 12,000 barrels of beer every year. It was located between Pearl (West Twenty-fifth) Street and Brainard Avenue, which today is near the western end of the Lorain-Carnegie Bridge and a block south of the West Side Market. In later years, Brainard was renamed Gehring Avenue.

Henry Hoffman and William Paschen established a small lager beer brewery on the city's southwest side in 1871. Located at the corner of Rhodes and Walton Avenues, the plant occupied a former clock factory. By 1878, the plant's annual capacity had reached 8,000 barrels, although actual production appears to have never been more than 3,000 barrels in any given year. Brewing operations ceased soon after Henry Hoffman's death in 1881. This drawing is from the *Cleveland City Atlas of 1874*.

BEREA BREWERY.

E. DAVIS,
Manufacturer of

Ales, Porter & Brown Stout.

WILL deliver ALES to Families and others in the village, free of charge, at the following prices:

Present Use XX Ale, per Bbl......$ 9 00

Old Stock Ale, per Bbl.............. 12 00

Cream Ale, per Bbl.................. 10 00

Kennett Ale, per Bbl............ ... . 14 00

Porter, per Bbl................ . ..... 12 00

Best Cream Ale, per ½ Cbl.... ...... 2 50

While the vast majority of the area's 19th-century brewers were in the city of Cleveland, suburban Berea had its own brewery, located on River Street (now Rocky River Drive), opposite Depot Street. Founded by Edward Davis in 1870, the plant was soon producing around 2,000 barrels of ale, porter, and stout each year. It changed owners numerous times over the next 20 years and was known as the North Shore Export Brewing Company when it burned to the ground in January 1897. This early advertisement for Davis's brews appeared in the *Grindstone City Advertiser*.

The oldest known photograph of a Cleveland brewery, this view from around 1870 was part of an advertisement showing the Forest City Brewery at 32–38 Irving (later East Twenty-fifth) Street. Founded in 1850 by Thomas Newman, it was one of three breweries in Cleveland to utilize the city's nickname. By the time of this photograph, the brewery was being operated by Newman and Daniel Fovargue, a recent arrival from Cambridge, England. Although the management of the small plant changed several times over the next decade, it produced around 3,000 barrels of ale and lager beer each year until its closing in 1883.

Leonhard Schlather was a native of Jebenhausen, Wurttemberg, Germany, who had come to America in 1853 and to Cleveland three years later. After working with fellow brewer and German immigrant Carl Gehring in the ale brewery of John M. Hughes, Schlather founded his own plant in 1857 for the production of lager beer, which was a relatively new beverage in the United States. Requiring a longer period of aging than ale, lager rapidly became the most popular type of beer in the country, and those who brewed it were often destined for great success.

In this photograph from 1875, Leonhard Schlather is seen with his employees at his original small, wooden frame brewery at 1903 West Twenty-eighth Street, in what is today known as Ohio City. The small brewery was producing more than 21,000 barrels of beer per year, making it the city's second largest at the time. Three years after this photograph was taken, continued growth forced Schlather to build a much larger plant.

Saloons were plentiful in Cleveland and most other cities in the 19th century. They provided beer and liquor, but more importantly, they provided social gathering places for the city's many immigrants, especially German ones. This saloon served Schlather Beer, as indicated by the large signs on either side of the entrance. In many cases, the saloon owner would live at the site with his family, and family photographs would often include views of the saloon, despite the unsavory reputation of such establishments. (Don Augenstein collection.)

This artist's rendering depicts the new, ornate Schlather brewery, which was built around the existing one in 1878. Made of brick and stone, it was the first of the city's breweries to move into the modern era of large-scale brewing operations. This image appeared in *The Western Brewer*, a brewing industry trade magazine, in 1880.

The photograph above shows the Schlather brewery as it appeared around the beginning of the century. The plant joined the large Cleveland and Sandusky Brewing Company combine in 1902 and continued to operate until the onset of Prohibition in 1919. Despite the magnificent architecture, the building was built specifically for brewing and had little use once brewing operations ended. It was leveled during the Prohibition era, and a supermarket stands at the site today.

This invoice from 1901 shows Schlather Beer being purchased by Ambrose Webber in East Liverpool, along the Ohio River. Schlather was a shrewd businessman; he not only owned a large number of saloons in Cleveland but also was tied to a large number of them in the Ohio River Valley, extending well into the southern part of the state. Webber continued to sell Schlather Beer even after becoming involved with the new Crockery City Brewing Company in East Liverpool.

This ornate serving tray dates to the 1890s. Trays were often used in saloons to advertise specific brands of beer, and many from that era were very detailed, often showing images of the breweries themselves. This particular tray is made of brass with a porcelain inlay in the center.

Although the Leisy brewery was phenomenally successful in the late 19th century, its origins were much simpler when it was founded in 1858 by Jacob Mueller. After the plant was sold in 1864 to Frederick Haltnorth, the proprietor of a larger beer garden in the city, it began to grow larger, producing 12,000 barrels by the early 1870s, when this photograph was taken. In 1873, Haltnorth sold the busy plant to Isaac, August, and Henry Leisy, three brothers from Friedelsheim, Bavaria, for $120,000. (Carl Miller collection.)

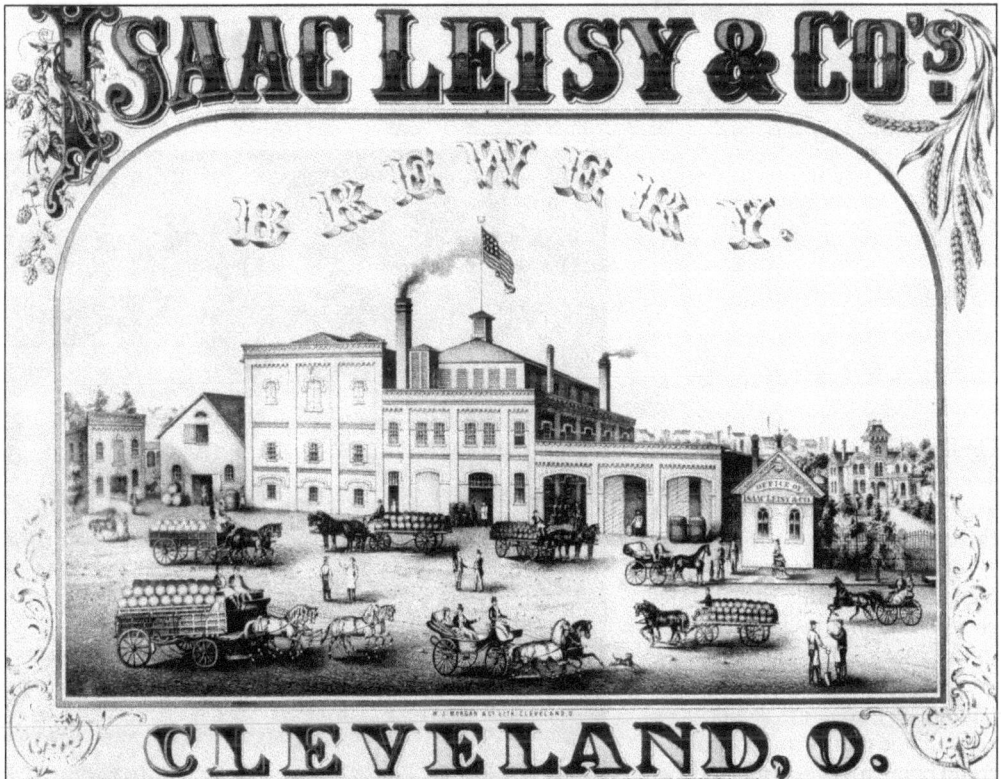

In this advertisement from 1876, there have been a few additions to the Leisy plant, allowing it to produce more than 24,000 barrels of beer a year and making it the city's largest brewery at the time. The company's tremendous success would necessitate a complete rebuilding of the plant within a few years. At the far right is the family's ornate Victorian home, which later served as the company's office and remained standing for nearly another century.

17

Isaac Leisy was a native of Friedelsheim, Bavaria, who had come to America as a teenager in 1855 with his family. Starting out with farming in rural Iowa, Leisy and two brothers moved to Keokuk, Iowa, where they successfully operated a brewery for several years before moving to Cleveland in 1873. In less than 20 years, he established a massive family brewing enterprise before his death in 1892 at age 54.

Underneath the Leisy brewery was a series of stone-lined caves that were used to cool and age beer in the early days. With the advent of mechanical refrigeration, beer could be successfully stored above ground in buildings known as stock houses. After the end of Prohibition, these caves were remodeled into a rathskeller, where large groups and visitors could come to eat, drink, and be merry. Here brewmaster Otto Kalsen (left) poses with engineer Julius Gisi in the rathskeller in 1951. (Cleveland State University Library collection.)

Weiss beer was a wheat-based, light-colored beer that had a small but loyal following among Cleveland's German population, although it never caught on with the general public in a big way. Several Weiss beer brewers existed in the city in the latter part of the 19th century, but the last one to operate was that of Carl E. Beltz, who had a small brewery behind his home on East Sixty-seventh Street, turning out several hundred barrels annually between 1905 and 1914. This photograph shows one of his delivery wagons. (Bill Carlisle collection.)

Cleveland had bottling depots for several large breweries that had widespread distribution even in the late 19th century. The Pabst, Schlitz, and Miller Brewing Companies of Milwaukee all had beer bottled in Cleveland, as did Anheuser-Busch of St. Louis. Other regional brewers sold beer in the city as well, most notably the Stroh Brewing Company of Detroit, which remained a favorite of Clevelanders as late as the 1980s. This turn-of-the-century, horse-drawn wagon delivered Stroh Beer to neighborhoods in the city. (Cleveland State University Library collection.)

Saloons were the primary outlet for beer sales prior to 1900, and many of the city's saloons were tied to one brewery or another during that period. A large sign like this would often hang outside the saloon, indicating the brand of beer sold inside. This *c.* 1898 photograph shows a saloon affiliated with the Cleveland Brewing Company, a large plant located on the city's far east side, within a few blocks of what is now University Circle. (Don Augenstein collection.)

The Shortstop saloon stood in downtown Cleveland in the 1890s. Like most of the city's saloons, it was affiliated with a brewery, specifically the Gehring Brewing Company. Even that early, large, nationally distributing companies were providing competition: on the side of the building, four doors down, is a large advertisement for Anheuser-Busch's Malt Nutrine, a nutritional supplement that first appeared in 1895. (Carl Miller collection.)

Employees of the Cleveland Brewing Company assembled for this photograph in 1887. Many breweries had these types of photographs taken during the era, showing all of the employees with the owners, who were usually well dressed at front and center. The various employees would frequently be holding their large brewing tools, and often a brewery mascot (usually a large dog) would also be included. This photograph was taken around the time that Ernst Mueller purchased the company and began to build it up from a small, rural brewery into a large and successful enterprise.

Andrew Oppmann was one of Cleveland's earliest true entrepreneur brewers. Purchasing a small brewery at the corner of Columbus and Willey Streets on the city's near west side in 1871, he gradually built it into a thriving company, until it was destroyed on July 4, 1889, by fireworks gone astray. It was soon rebuilt, however, and later became part of the Cleveland and Sandusky Brewing Company combine. Here Oppmann (front row, to the right of the barrels) and his employees pose in October 1880. (Harvey G. Oppmann collection.)

Wenzl Medlin was a native of Bohemia (today part of the Czech Republic), who had come to America in 1866 at age 17. After moving to Cleveland in 1886, he operated the Bohemian Brewery on Pearl (West Twenty-fifth) Street for several years before leaving to found the new Medlin Pilsener Brewing Company, which would later produce the venerable P.O.C. brand of beer. Medlin left there in 1899 to operate a very small Weiss beer brewery at his home for a few more years before dying in 1912.

This photograph shows the former plant of the Kress Weiss Brewing Company, a small Weiss beer brewery operated by Andrew Kress at Sackett and West Thirty-second Streets, around 1904. Smaller breweries like this would show employees posing in front of the plant, often with a wagon loaded with barrels nearby. Kress made Weiss beer in the plant between 1902 and 1903 before it was purchased by a new group of saloon owners who renamed it the Standard Brewing Company (as shown here on the wagon). In late 1904, however, Standard moved to a larger site in a former flour mill, and this small plant by another new group that renamed it again, this time as the Excelsior Brewing Company, after which a complete expansion and modernization of the plant took place. (Bill Carlisle collection.)

Established in 1870, the brewery at the southeast corner of Train and West Forty-Seventh Streets was operated throughout most of its history by Christian Schneider and his son John. After being destroyed by a lightning strike, which set the plant ablaze in 1891, it was rebuilt completely and, in 1895, was purchased by a new group that renamed it the Union Brewing Company. It was incorporated into the Cleveland and Sandusky Brewing Company combine in 1898 and subsequently closed in 1902. The plant has had several additions over the years and housed an ice cream manufacturer at one point. It remains standing to this day.

Jacob Baehr was a German immigrant who had worked with the Leisy brothers at their brewery in Iowa before coming to Cleveland in 1866. He then established a brewery on Pearl (West Twenty-fifth) Street, while his wife, Magdalena, operated a saloon in the front of the building and their eight children lived upstairs. Baehr died in 1873, after which his wife continued to operate the plant until it was purchased by the Cleveland and Sandusky Brewing Company combine in 1898. The plant was closed in 1901. This photograph shows the remodeled brewery today, still retaining its original smokestack in the rear.

Two

THE RISE OF
CORPORATE BREWERIES
1890s–1919

The origins of the Cleveland Brewing Company date back to 1852, when it was established by Robert Hoffman and C. W. Schmidt. The small original plant was on the city's far east side at Hough and Ansel Avenues, overlooking what is now Rockefeller Park, near University Circle. Several additions over the years built it into one of the city's largest breweries before it was purchased by the Cleveland and Sandusky Brewing Company in 1898. Production at the site ended with Prohibition in 1919. (Carl Miller collection.)

TELEPHON: Bell East 611 J. Cuyahoga R. 568.

THE BELTZ ✳ BREWING CO.

JOS. BELTZ PRES. & TREAS.

VAL. KOENIG VICE. PRES.

L. C. BELTZ SEC.

JOHN J. BELTZ SUPT. & MGR.

Feines Lagerbier, Ale, Stout und Weissbier.

Ecke Slater und Outhwaite Avenue.

Cleveland, O.

The Beltz Brewing Company evolved from the tiny Weiss beer brewery operated for more than 20 years by Joseph Beltz. Located at the corner of East Sixty-first Street and Outhwaite Avenue, the company was incorporated in 1901, when lager beer production began, after which operations began to expand dramatically. Largely a family operation to this point, the company was taken over in 1907 by Ernst Mueller, formerly of the Cleveland and Sandusky Brewing Company. At that time, it was renamed as the Cleveland Home Brewing Company. This advertisement is from the *Wachter und Unzeiger*, the city's German-language newspaper, in 1902. (Bill Carlisle collection.)

The Diebolt Brewing Company
Brauerei und Flaſchenbier-Geſchäft.
PITTSBURG STR., Ecke Jackſon.   CLEVELAND, O.

Obgleich die Diebolt Brewing Co. erſt dieſes Jahr incorporirt wurde, iſt dieſelbe doch ſchon beiläufig 40 Jahre in Exiſtenz und flottem Betrieb. Die Beamten dieſer Company ſind: A. J. Diebolt, Präſ.; J. A. Diebolt, Vicepräſ.; W. L. Diebolt, Sekr. und Schatzmeiſter. Das in jeder Hinſicht nach modernem Stil eingerichtete Etabliſſement erſtreckt ſich an der Frontſeite auf 476 Fuß und an der anderen Seite auf 138 Fuß; die Frontſeite an der Jackſon-Straße iſt 140 Fuß lang. ✳ ✳ ✳ ✳ ✳

und Hotelgebrauch fabrizirt. — Dies iſt eine der im erfreulichſten Aufſchwung befindlichen Brauereien dieſer Stadt und die raſch zunehmende Kundſchaft iſt hauptſächlich den praktiſchen und liberalen Methoden ihrer Geſchäftsleitung wie der Vorzüglichkeit ihrer Produkte zuzuſchreiben. ✳ ✳ ✳ ✳ ✳

Die Produktionsfähigkeit der Brauerei beläuft ſich jährlich auf 75,000 Faß und die feinen Qualitäten ihres reinen Lagerbieres ſind als rühmenswerthe Spezialitäten allſeits bekannt und beliebt.

Zu dem ſchon vor ungefähr acht Jahren etablirten Flaſchenbiergeſchäft werden verſchiedene Sorten, wie „White Seal", „Böhmiſches Export" und „Standard Lager" für den Familien-

This large advertisement for the Diebolt Brewing Company appeared in the *Wachter und Unzeiger* in 1902. Even after the dawn of the century, many Cleveland residents still primarily used their native languages, and German-language newspapers continued to operate until the onset of World War I, when anti-German sentiment made many of them attempt to hide their heritage. (Bill Carlisle collection.)

The Gund Brewing Co.
Die Brauerei wurde im Jahre 1860 durch die Herren Rindsvater und Mall etablirt und ſpäter unter dem Namen „The Jacob Mall Brewing Company" weitergeführt, welche unter dieſem Namen im Jahre 1889 incorporirt wurde.

Am erſten April 1897 wurde die Brauerei von Herrn Geo. F. Gund käuflich übernommen und hat ſich dieſelbe unter deſſen umſichtiger Leitung zu einer der erſten Brauereien dieſer Stadt emporgeſchwungen.

Sein Beſtreben war, ein erſter Klaſſe Bier auf den Markt zu bringen und es zeigt ſich, daß er dieſen Zweck vollſtändig erreichte, da die Verkäufe ſich während dieſer Zeit derart vermehrten, daß die Firma gezwungen war, bedeutende Vergrößerungen an deren Etabliſſement vorzunehmen. Auch wurde ein Flaſchenbiergeſchäft eingerichtet und deſſen berühmtes „Gund's Cryſtal Bottled Beer" ſucht ſeines Gleichen.

Die erſt vor kurzem vollendeten feuerſicheren Stallungen zählen zu den beſten in dieſem Staate.

Am 1. Januar 1900 wurde der Name der Brauerei in den „The Gund Brewing Company" umgeändert. Die Beamten und Direktoren ſind die folgenden Herren:

Geo. F. Gund, Präſ. und Schatzm;
G. A. Kaercher, Vicepräſident;
Jacob Fickel, Sekretär;
F. C. Heiss,
Geo. Zimmerman.

Herr Gund war früher mit der John Gund Brewing Co. in La Croſſe, Wis., verbunden und übernahm ſpäter die Leitung der „Seattle Brewing & Malting Company" in Seattle, Waſh., welcher er als Präſident bis 1897 vorſtand.

This is another advertisement from the *Wachter und Unzeiger*, this one for the Gund Brewing Company. In this drawing, Lake Erie is behind the brewery, which stood at a site known as Davenport Bluffs, overlooking what is now the Cleveland Shoreway (State Route 2) and Burke Lakefront Airport. The site is now occupied by the television studios of WKYC-Channel 3.

Kellersaft

O Kellersaft!

Du edler Tropfen
Aus bestem Malz
Und feinstem Hopfen!
Du schaffst Humor,
Du schaffst auch Kraefte,
Du edelster
Der Gerstensaefte!
D'rum trink' ich dich,
Mein Ein', mein Alles,—
Ob ich bei Geld,
Ob ich den Dalles,—
Als Medizin
Wie als Getraenke,
Zu Haus' sowohl,
Wie in der Schenke.

Beſtellt per Telephon:

Bell, Weſt 115

Cuyahoga, Central 5955

✳

frei ins Haus geliefert

Das
beſte der Flaſchenbiere.

✳

In der Brauerei abgezogen.

✳

Beſtes Malz und deutſcher
Hopfen.

Kellersaft Beer was introduced in 1905 by the Cleveland and Sandusky Brewing Company. The name meant "cellar juice" in German and was chosen through a contest in which local residents submitted potential names. The winning entry came from a local minister, who won $100 for his efforts. This German-language advertisement appeared in a program for a musical concert held at Grays' Armory, February 17, 1907.

The Pilsener Brewing Company

Brauer von

EXTRA PILSENER BIER.

Beamte:

Vaclav Hladik, Präsident.
Carl Anders, Vice Präs.
Kar. Humel, Kaſſirer und
Geſchäftsführer.
Jos. C. Wolf, Sekr.

Direktoren:

Vaclav Hladik,
Vac. Humel,
Carl Anders,
H. G. Rudolph,
Frank Marek,
Adolph Humel,
Chas. Bruml,
John Kratochvil,
Jas. C. Wolf.

Another advertisement from the *Wachter und Unzeiger*, in 1903, shows the Pilsener Brewing Company and its directors as of 1903. From left to right are (top) John (Frank) Kratochvil, Henry G. Rudolph, and Charles Bruml; (middle) Vaclav Humel, Vaclav Hladik, and Carl Anders; (bottom) Frank Marek, James C. Wolf, and Adolph F. Humel. In its early days, the Pilsener brewery's primary market was the large European immigrant population on the city's west side. Its anchor brand, P.O.C. Beer, was popular with both Czechs and Germans.

The Forest City Brewing Company was formed in 1904 by Bohemian/Czech immigrants Michael Albl and Joseph F. Troyan. The new company's location at 6900 Union Avenue on the city's near southeast side was near Slavic Village, a district heavily populated with eastern European immigrants. Pictured here is a message on the company's letterhead from company treasurer Vaclav Humel, written in the native Czech language.

This photograph shows the plant of the Forest City Brewing Company soon after opening. The towers and gables were very typical of industrial architecture in the era, taking the ornate Victorian architecture seen in breweries 20 years earlier to new levels. As was typical of large breweries built after the dawn of the century, the building's supports and all of the brewery's vessels (fermenting tanks, aging casks, and so forth) were of steel construction instead of wood, making the plant far more fire resistant than earlier breweries. It featured a five-story brew house with a 225-barrel kettle, yielding an annual capacity of 50,000 barrels, and the cost of construction was estimated at $220,000.

Like the city's other brewers, Forest City owned saloons, which would primarily serve that brewery's beers. Since many saloon owners lived on the premises, it was not unusual for photographs of their children to show them standing next to beer signs or bottles or kegs of beer and liquor. This photograph was taken around 1910. (Don Augenstein collection.)

Soon after the beginning of the century, gasoline-powered trucks began to replace horse-drawn beer wagons, and by 1910, the majority of the city's beer delivery vehicles were motor driven. Each brewery had its own fleet of trucks, such as this chain-driven model seen leaving the Forest City brewery about 1915. (Courtesy of John Murray.)

The small brewery on Sackett Avenue was purchased by brewmaster Jacob Haller and renamed as the Excelsior Brewing Company in 1905. It was soon rebuilt with a modern three-story brewhouse, which brought its annual capacity up to 30,000 barrels. However, this still left it as one of the city's smallest breweries. The company was known for its Excelsior Success and Golden Seal Beers, and it continued to operate throughout the Prohibition era as the Eilert Beverage Company, producing nonalcoholic beer and soft drinks. After Repeal in 1933, it was renamed as the Eilert Brewing Company. The building remains standing today, although the top floor was removed at some point. (Bill Carlisle collection.)

Taken around 1915, this image shows a delivery truck for the Excelsior Brewing Company. Like most of the city's breweries that opened after the beginning of the century, Excelsior focused on home sales of bottled beer instead of exclusively selling kegged beer to saloons like most of the older established breweries had done. (Carl Miller collection.)

The Lion brewery, originally owned by Paul Kindsvater and Jacob Mall, stood on Davenport Avenue, just east of downtown. It was incorporated as the Jacob Mall Brewing Company in 1889, two years before Mall's death. Incorporation gave the company capital to completely rebuild and modernize the brewery through the 1890s, culminating with the addition of a four-story brew house in 1896. This gave the plant an annual capacity of 30,000 barrels, most of it being the popular Mall's Crystal Lager Beer. One year later, the plant was sold to George F. Gund. (Bill Carlisle collection.)

The Gund Brewing Company was very successful throughout its existence, remaining in operation until statewide Prohibition took effect in 1919. Although still owned by the Gund Realty Company (formed to manage saloon properties in the city), the brewery was largely vacated for several years before housing a small malt syrup company in 1927. Upon the repeal of Prohibition, the brewery was modernized and reopened as the Sunrise Brewing Company, remaining in business until 1944. This photograph is from the 1930s, after Sunrise was in business. (Carl Miller collection.)

Many breweries in the pre-Prohibition era used trade cards to advertise their products. This c. 1905 trade card for the Gund Brewing Company is shaped like a crate filled with bottles of Gund's Crystal Lager Beer.

Gund's Crystal Lager was the company's best-selling brand at the beginning of the century, but it was joined by Ye Old Lager around 1904. This is a die-cut bottle label for the latter brand.

George F. Gund was the son of John Gund, owner of the large John Gund Brewing Company of LaCrosse, Wisconsin. George had worked for his father and later moved West, where he became the president of the Seattle Brewing and Malting Company. In 1897, at the age of 42, he returned to the Midwest to purchase Cleveland's Jacob Mall Brewing Company, renaming it three years later as the Gund Brewing Company and starting to build a financial empire. An entrepreneur in the truest sense of the word, he used money generated by the brewery to invest in other ventures, such as mining companies, realty, and banking. He had been on the boards of two banks in Seattle and was associated with two in Cleveland as well. Gund died in 1916 at age 60.

This ornate advertising sign from around 1900 was made for Gund by the Meyercord Company. It consists of a decal on a thin sheet of plywood. At the time, beer was not sold in grocery stores or carryout stores; most was sold in saloons or directly from the brewery to a consumer's home. Therefore, nearly all advertising signs like this hung on the walls of saloons or restaurants.

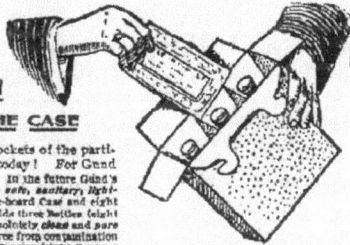

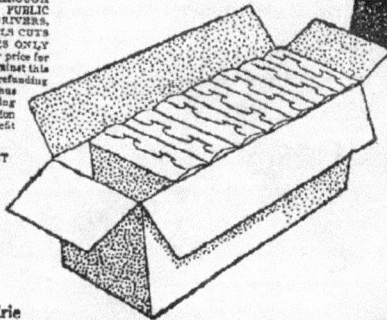

This large advertisement appeared in the *Cleveland Plain Dealer* on January 4, 1912, introducing Gund's Finest Beer to the public. This would remain as the company's anchor brand for the next seven years. The advertisement also focused on the unique packing of the bottles in individual wrappers and then in cartons of three and crates of 24. Gund also utilized coupons for those who bought beer in cases to take part in profit sharing, where coupons could be redeemed for various household goods such as appliances, silverware, and furniture, all listed in a large catalog.

This view of the Gund brewery is from the shore of Lake Erie, showing the bluff on which the brewery stood. The site had been chosen in 1850 by brewery founder Martin Stumpf to allow for building underground lagering cellars in the hillside and also because it allowed for easy access to the lake for cutting ice in the winter. In later years, the shoreline was extended north to allow for the construction of the Cleveland Shoreway and Burke Lakefront Airport. The brewery remained standing until the 1960s. (Carl Miller collection.)

Shortly after George F. Gund died in 1916, his son George II moved from Seattle to manage the brewery's operations. He soon introduced Gund's Clevelander Beer, which was quickly met with good local sales. Showing an older gentleman who represented Moses Cleaveland, the city's founder, viewing the city's public square and the famous Soldiers and Sailors Monument (built in 1894), the brand's bottle label was one of the city's most graphic ever.

George Gund II assumed control of the family brewery in 1916, but less than three years later, Prohibition brought beer production to a halt. Despite this, he continued to operate the associated Gund Realty Company and successfully invested his money elsewhere, eventually serving as president of the Cleveland Trust Company, the state's largest bank. By the time of his death in 1966, he was worth $600 million and was considered to be the wealthiest man in Cleveland. Today the family fortune is estimated at $1.6 billion. (Cleveland State University Library collection.)

Perhaps the most visible legacy of Cleveland's brewing history is the 20,500-seat Gund Arena, opened in 1994 and located in the Gateway District of downtown. Built mainly for the NBA's Cleveland Cavaliers basketball team, the arena also has been home to minor league hockey games and many rock concerts, ice shows, and other events. George Gund III and brother Gordon were the owners of the Cavaliers for more than 20 years, and they had the arena's original naming rights. After they sold the team in 2005, it was renamed the Quicken Loans Arena.

Established in 1867, the Star Brewery was located on Buckley Street near West Forty-first Street. After several years, it came into the ownership of George V. Muth, who built it into a successful company. In 1885, the plant was rebuilt as the modern three-story brick structure shown here. New ownership in 1895 renamed it the Star Brewing Company, which was purchased by the Cleveland and Sandusky Brewing Company in 1898. It continued to operate until 1913, when it was permanently closed. (Carl Miller collection.)

The origins of the Columbia Brewery date to 1859, when Joseph Stoppel founded it in the city's Flats district. In 1887, it was rebuilt two blocks away, on the Commercial Street hillside. The plant was purchased by the Cleveland and Sandusky Brewing Company in 1898, and continued to operate until November 1918, when statewide Prohibition was voted into effect.

38

Die Brauerei der Standard Brewing Co.

Germans and Bohemians were not the only ethnic groups involved in Cleveland's brewing industry. Men of Irish descent (Stephen S. Creadon and John T. Feighan) were responsible for the formation of the Standard Brewing Company on the city's west side in 1903. One year after starting operations, the company moved to a new site at a former flour mill on Train Avenue, where it would continue to do business until 1961. Seen here is an architect's drawing of the plant after being refitted and enlarged for brewing.

Stephen S. Creadon was a saloon owner and was well aware of the plight of the city's other saloon owners, who were being financially manipulated in the 1890s and early 20th century by the city's breweries, most of whom had been locked in fierce competition for the past decade and were using the small saloons as pawns in the battle to sell their beers. Following a trend in many other cities in Ohio and the rest of the country, Creadon and Feighan formed a company in which the majority of stock was held by saloon owners. Beer brewed here would be sold in their saloons, allowing them to escape the economic control of the city's larger brewers. Creadon died in 1921 at age 55.

The Standard Brewing Company had originally kept a large fleet of horse-drawn delivery wagons, but after several years, these had largely been replaced by trucks. Here crates of the company's flagship brand, Erin Brew (also called Ehren Brau so as not to alienate German customers), are loaded precariously onto a delivery truck around 1915. (Courtesy of the American Truck Historical Society.)

The Diebolt Brewing Company stood at 2702 Pittsburgh Street, atop a steep hill overlooking a main span of railroad tracks. Although the brewery's origins could be traced back to 1856, the Diebolt brothers (Anthony, Joseph, Mathias, and Frank) became involved with the company in 1888, after which its production increased dramatically; its annual capacity eventually reached 80,000 barrels. Shown here are two delivery trucks outside the plant's loading dock around 1914. (Carl Miller collection.)

Like most of the city's breweries, the Diebolt Brewing Company bottled an increasing percentage of its beer for home sales in the decade prior to Prohibition. Part of the reason was that as the temperance forces gained power, saloons were increasingly coming under attack as havens for drunkenness and illegal activity. Therefore, many breweries felt that by distancing themselves from the saloon trade, they might stave off Prohibition. In 1915, Diebolt built an entirely new bottling plant, which featured this modern soaking machine (as seen in the trade magazine *The Western Brewer*) to clean and sterilize all bottles before being filled.

Diebolt's White Seal Beer was the company's flagship brand, advertised as "the Triumph of Brewing," and was sold along with Diebolt's Standard Beer (a bottle label of which appears here), Bohemian Export, Malt Tonic, and, of course, Bock beer in the spring. All were brewed under the supervision of brewmaster Paul Hohman.

The Diebolt stable building stood on the north side of Pittsburgh Avenue, across the street from the rest of the brewery complex, and remained standing until 1979. The structure was even more imposing in appearance than the rest of the brewery, resembling a large fortress more than a stable. A large concrete horse head stood out above the main doorway until the end. A large branch of the United States Postal Service stands at the site today.

THE I. LEISY BREWING CO.
CLEVELAND, OHIO.

CAPACITY 500,000 BARRELS

This trade card is from the 1890s and shows an artist's rendering of the Leisy brewery (most of which was built in 1883 and 1884), facing Vega Avenue. While there is some degree of exaggeration in the drawing, it does show a general layout of the plant. In the foreground at left are the stables, which were razed for the construction of Interstate 90, running parallel to Vega Avenue today. In the foreground at right is the mansion built by Isaac Leisy, finished in 1892. In reality, an older Victorian frame home used as son Otto Leisy's home stood at that site, while Isaac's mansion stood farther to the right (out of the picture). In addition, the large building in the background never existed; it is merely a view of the rear of the plant, shown in the following photograph.

While the Leisy brewery and grounds were designed to look ornate and beautiful to passersby on Vega Avenue, this c. 1915 view from the rear side of the plant facing the railroad tracks was very different, with a typical industrial appearance. While the majority of the plant was razed in 1974, the smokestack at far left remains standing today, as do the lower two floors of the section at far right, visible from Train Avenue.

This *c.* 1912 photograph shows a scene inside the Leisy bottling plant. While the bottling process was becoming increasingly mechanized, it was still fairly labor intensive, not to mention dangerous by today's standards. Flywheels and conveyor belts were constantly in motion without any safety features, and serious injuries were fairly common throughout the early breweries. (Bill Carlisle collection.)

Leisy's sales continued to grow rapidly throughout the pre-Prohibition era: 100,000 barrels sold in 1898; 300,000 barrels in 1913; and over 565,000 barrels in 1918 (representing full capacity for the facility). Home sales of bottled beer continued to grow as well, making up 30 percent of the plant's output by 1917. Accordingly, a large bottling plant was built in 1915 across Fulton Avenue from the main complex, and an additional facility was built two years later. This photograph (from *The Western Brewer* magazine in 1915) shows a modern bottle-filling machine inside the Leisy brewery.

This illustration shows one of several different types of delivery trucks used by Leisy in the decade prior to Prohibition. This particular photograph was taken from a catalog for the Gramm-Bernstein Motor Truck Company of Lima, Ohio, and gives an example of their 5–6 ton category of trucks.

On the far east end of the Leisy brewery complex was Isaac Leisy's own home, completed in 1892, shortly before his death. A large, three-story brownstone mansion, it had several gables and copper-plated towers, which were typical of the era, and it served as the crowning touch to a brewery, which was characterized by style just as much as it was known for the high quality of beer produced within. As was the case with many of Cleveland's huge, ornate Victorian mansions, its upkeep in later years was unaffordable, and once the last family member had moved out of the home in the 1940s, it was razed. (Cleveland State University Library collection.)

Ornate serving trays continued to be a commonly seen item in the city's saloons, providing function as well as marketing. Today they are highly sought-after collectibles. The large eagle and six-sided brewer's star remained as the company's symbols throughout its existence. The brewer's star was used by many German immigrant brewers, and while identical to the Star of David, it was not an indication of the brewer's religion. In fact, the Leisy family were Mennonites.

Die Cleveland Home Brauerei.

The Beltz Brewing Company evolved out of Joseph Beltz's small Weiss beer brewery on the city's east side. Its business rapidly improved after it was incorporated in 1901, and soon after that, the plant was completely rebuilt, increasing the annual capacity from 10,000 to 75,000 barrels. This architect's drawing of the new plant appeared in 1907 in *Cleveland und Sein Deutschthum*, a book detailing many of the city's prominent Germans. That same year, the company reincorporated as the Cleveland Home Brewing Company, which remained in business until 1952.

This view from 1914 shows the Pilsener Brewing Company plant, located at 6605 Clark Avenue. Originally built in 1892 by Bohemian immigrant Wenzl Medlin, the plant was owned and operated entirely by Bohemians such as Vaclav Humel, Jaro Pavlik, Vinzenz Spietschka, and Zdenek Sobotka. The name Pilsener referred to a style of beer made famous in Plzen (Pilsen), Czechoslovakia, although the name is used today in a more generic form to refer to a particular (and popular) type of lager beer. After a change in ownership in 1935, the company remained in business until 1962.

Employees of the Pilsener Brewing Company pose in front of the plant around 1905. It is not unusual to see teenagers or children in these photographs, as child labor laws were largely nonexistent at the time. It is more likely, however, that this small child was the son of one of the company's directors. (Courtesy of Bob Bickford and Carl Miller.)

This is one of several different types of delivery trucks used by the Pilsener Brewing Company around 1915. In addition to the flagship P.O.C. brand of beer, the company also produced Extra Pilsener Gold Top and Zunt Heit beers. Bottles of Gold Top beer came with gold foil over the bottle cap, like champagne. (Don Augenstein collection.)

Through most of the Pilsener Brewing Company's existence, its flagship brand was P.O.C. Beer. Although the company never admitted what the initials stood for, it was widely assumed they meant Pride of Cleveland or Pilsener of Cleveland, or words to that effect. This metal sign was typical of advertisements seen in the city's saloons. The "Sixth City" is a reference to Cleveland being the sixth-largest city (by population) in the country at the time. (Bill Carlisle collection.)

After a disastrous fire in 1889 that leveled Andrew Oppmann's wooden-frame brewery just south of the Flats district, it was rebuilt as a large and ornate plant (shown above) that increased the Oppmann Brewing Company's annual capacity to 50,000 barrels. When Oppmann sold the plant two years later, the new group renamed it as the Phoenix Brewing Company, symbolizing the company's rising from the ashes just like the mythological bird of the same name. The company became part of the Cleveland and Sandusky Brewing Company combine in 1898, and it continued to operate until closing permanently in 1908. It was later razed, leaving no remains today. To the right is a large metal sign advertising the brewery. (Bill Carlisle collection.)

After its founding in 1857, the Gehring Brewing Company was rebuilt and enlarged in 1876 and again in 1885, after which it appeared as in the drawing shown here. The enlargements allowed it to achieve 90,000 barrels of annual production by the end of the century, making it the city's third-largest brewery. When it joined the Cleveland and Sandusky Brewing Company in 1898, it was the largest in the group, and its 95 employees accounted for one-third of the workforce in the entire company. The plant continued to operate until 1918, when Prohibition closed it down. It burned and was razed in 1927.

Simon Fishel was a native of Bohemia, born in 1846, who had come to America as a young adult after learning the brewing trade in Europe. Starting at the Bohemian Brewing Company on the city's west side in the 1880s, he later formed the Fishel Brewing Company on East Fifty-fifth Avenue, which was then purchased by the Cleveland and Sandusky Brewing Company in 1907. Fishel became president of the large combine and remained in that position until his death in 1917. One of the city's first Jewish brewers, Fishel was active in the city's Jewish community, being one of the founders of the Euclid Avenue Temple, of which he was president, and a director of the city's Montefiore Jewish home.

The Cleveland and Sandusky Brewing Company was formed in 1898 when the owners of nine breweries in Cleveland (Baehr, Barrett, Bohemian, Cleveland, Columbia, Gehring, Phoenix, Star, and Union), along with the Kuebeler and Stang breweries in Sandusky, merged as one company to avoid the pitfalls of competition (price wars, advertising, and so forth) between rival brewers, allowing the constituent members to pool their resources, save money, and share the wealth. Another advantage of the merger, although unstated, was that the large combine would have a dramatic competitive advantage over smaller companies that had not joined it. It would later include the Schlather, Fishel, and Lorain Brewing Companies as well. Among the many brands of bottled beer that were produced by the company were White Label and Bohemian, as shown on this tin sign made in Coshocton, Ohio, around 1915. (Bill Carlisle collection.)

This painting shows Ernst Mueller, who had one of the longest and most illustrious careers of any Cleveland brewer. Born in Alsenz, Bavaria, in 1851, he came to America as a child and for many years worked in his father's malting business, Peter Mueller and Company, which was one of the largest in Cleveland. Joining the Cleveland Brewing Company in 1887, he later became president of the Cleveland and Sandusky Brewing Company. After leaving the large combine due to internal politics in 1907, he became president of the Cleveland Home Brewing Company, remaining there through most of the Prohibition era until his death in 1931 at age 79.

ORDER A CASE OF
GOLD BOND BEER
$500⁰⁰ GOLD BOND BEER
THE FISHEL BREWING CO.
HARVARD 1400   CENTRAL 3933

$500⁰⁰ GOLD BOND BEER
This is to Certify
THAT
FISHEL BOND BEER

THE CLEVELAND & SANDUSKY BREWING CO.

Fishel's $500 Bond Beer appeared in Cleveland as soon as Simon Fishel's brewery opened in early 1905. The name was a reference to a promise (on the bottle label) by Fishel himself that anyone who could prove that "injurious substitutes" for the finest ingredients were used in the brewing process would be paid $500. The name was later changed to $500 Gold Bond Beer and still later to Gold Bond Beer, a name which would last for more than fifty years. This small cardboard wall sign dates to 1910. (Bill Carlisle collection.)

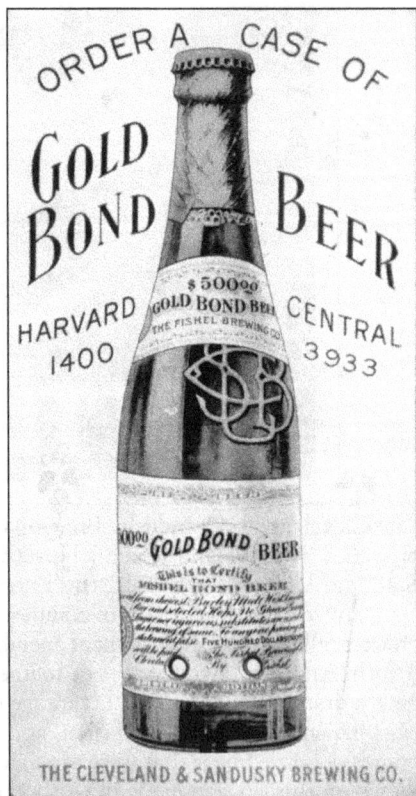

Culmbacher Lager Beer was another of Cleveland and Sandusky's many brands of bottled beer. Representing a style of lager made in Kulmbach, Germany, this label featured a drawing of King Gambrinus, who was also known as King John I of Flanders and was considered the patron saint of beer and brewing. This symbol was shared by many other brewers across the country, including Cleveland's Leisy Brewing Company, which had a statue of the king outside of its plant.

This advertisement for Clicco-Brew Beer appeared in the *Cleveland Plain Dealer* in November 1914. The advertising for the brand was criticized by writers for *The Western Brewer* trade magazine, who felt that it featured particularly festive social scenes, suggesting inebriation instead of moderation in drinking, and that this sort of depiction was encouraging the prohibitionists in their battle against all forms of alcohol. True or not, the brand was relatively short-lived.

As early as 1917, Leisy released a nonalcoholic malt beverage called Bevera, hoping to maintain sales in dry territories and protect its share of the beer market, if Prohibition were to occur. Advertised heavily throughout Ohio, the brand was available virtually everywhere that soda and other nonalcoholic beverages were sold. As was the case with most of the other cereal beverages made during the early 1920s, Bevera met with very poor sales. This was felt by some to have been the result of Cleveland's proximity to Canada, allowing easy access to bootlegged Canadian beer. Sales remained disappointing until the brewery closed its doors in 1923. The remaining stock of Bevera, 6,000 barrels in all, was poured down the sewer.

Three

PROHIBITION
1919–1933

After more than 40 years of organized opposition to alcohol, the country's prohibitionists succeeded in making all alcohol production illegal with the passage of the 18th Amendment to the Constitution, known as the Volstead Act. It outlawed the production and sale of beverages containing more than 0.5 percent alcohol, with few exceptions. The amendment went into effect January 17, 1920, after which time the entire country was officially dry. Ohio had a head start when residents voted the state dry after the November 1918 elections; alcohol sales in the state ceased in May 1919. Several years later, the Fishel brewery's brew kettle, shown here, sat unused. Someone had scrawled "We want beer" in the kettle's dust. (Cleveland State University Library collection.)

In May 1919, as statewide Prohibition took effect, the Diebolt Brewing Company continued in the ice business while introducing nonalcoholic Perlex Beverage. Like many of the city's other near-beer offerings, sales of this were poor, and all beverage production ceased in 1923.

While the Prohibition era would prove to be disastrous for the brewing industry, Cleveland and Sandusky's management remained optimistic at the outset that sales of cereal beverages could be successful, and that the saloon business might survive without serving alcohol. Along those lines, the company produced several brands of near beer, including old favorites Crystal Rock, Starlight, and Gold Bond, as well as new names such as Bola, Fifty-Fifty (made by contract for a national distribution network), and New York Special Brew (a label of which is shown here).

56

Bola beverage was one of Cleveland and Sandusky's more popular nonalcoholic beers and was sold throughout the northern part of Ohio. This advertisement appeared in the *Columbus Dispatch* on May 26, 1919, the first day that alcohol sales were prohibited. In addition, a number of noncereal soft drinks were bottled by the company, most notably Whistle Orange drink, Brownie Chocolate drink, Crystal Rock Water, Deerfield and Tommy-Green Ginger Ales, and Johnny Bull Ginger Beer.

Bola

THE GOLD BOND BEVERAGE

Between dances—drink cool, foaming, sparkling Bola—the drink with the jazzy zip—that says, "Have another?"

Ask for Bola at Soda Fountains and Stores

The Geo. Bobb & Sons Co.,
Sole Distributors
32 E. Main Street,   Columbus, Ohio

LEISY'S DRINKS
hot day comfort

After May 1919, the Leisy Brewing Company continued to produce Bevera along with five additional beverages: Leisy Premium Beverage (near beer), Leisy Old Fashioned Root Beer, Loganberry Beverage, Superior Orangeade, and Ginger Ale. This advertisement appeared in the *Cleveland Plain Dealer* in July 1920. Due to poor sales, all beverage production ended in 1923 as the plant shut down, although the Leisy family continued to make money through the Pontiac Improvement Company, established in 1914 to manage the brewery's extensive real estate holdings.

Built in 1904, the Fishel brewery (shown here about 1930) was one of the newest plants in the city, and when Prohibition began, it was one of only three plants owned by Cleveland and Sandusky that remained open (the Schlather brewery on the city's west side and the Stang brewery in Sandusky were the others). Sales of cereal beverages were disappointing, however, and by 1922, the Fishel plant had closed, with soft drink production being limited to the Schlather bottling plant. At Prohibition's end in 1933, the Schlather plant closed and the Fishel plant was reopened for brewing. (Carl Miller collection.)

One particularly successful Prohibition story involves George Gund II, whose brewery had recently shut down operations in early 1919 when he purchased the local Kaffee Hag (German for "coffee grove") Company. Intrigued by its formula for making decaffeinated coffee without destroying the taste, he spent $130,000 on the venture. As the company grew quickly, Gund sold the company eight years later to the Kellogg's Company of Michigan for $10 million, forming much of the basis for the family's fortune. Years later, the product was sold to General Foods, which renamed it Sanka. This advertisement is from *National Geographic*, September 1928. At the time, the company's headquarters were still on Davenport Avenue near the old brewery.

Kaffee Hag Coffee

has brought a new conception of sleep

COMPLETE sleep! It is not a question of hours—but of relaxation. It comes when muscles are at ease and nerves are reposed. Many used to give up the pleasure of coffee because they felt that caffeine affected nerves and sleep.

But nowadays, people are simply changing their coffee brand to a pure, delightful coffee that is 97% free of caffeine — Kaffee Hag Coffee.

And they don't forego a single delight! Kaffee Hag is a blend of the world's finest coffees. All the strength, all the cheery coffee flavor, is present. Only the tasteless, odorless caffeine is gone.

You'll say you've never tasted finer coffee. And you can enjoy a strong cup even at midnight—it will not affect nerves or rest. Doctors recommend it. How much better than substitutes!

Full-pound freshly sealed cans at your dealer's. Ground or in the bean. Order at hotels, restaurants. On dining-cars. For 10c we will send you a generous sample. And with it a booklet on *complete sleep*. Mail the coupon.

REMAIN AWAKE 115 HOURS IN TEST

Chicago Scientists Suffer Agonies in Study of Effects of Wakefulness

FIRST DAY WAS EASY

KAFFEE HAG CORPORATION
1810 Davenport Ave., Cleveland, Ohio

Please send me, postpaid, enough Kaffee Hag to make ten cups of good coffee. I enclose ten cents (stamps or coin).

Name____

Address____

KAFFEE HAG COFFEE

the COFFEE
that lets you sleep

The Pilsener Brewing Company remained in business throughout the Prohibition era, renamed as the Pilsener Products Company and then as the Pilsener Ice, Fuel and Beverage Company after 1928. Production of beer gave way to the production of several varieties of nonalcoholic P.O.C. "special brew" and "foaming beverage," as well as several varieties of soft drinks (ginger ale, parfay, and so on), still under the supervision of brewmaster Frank Knopp. The company survived the era much more successfully than most of its local competition and, in fact, was the only brewery in the city still producing near beer when Prohibition ended in 1933. This is a small wall sign for P.O.C. Parfay from around 1928. (Carl Miller collection.)

The Diebolt brothers' brewery had shut down in 1923; that facility and its ice plant were then taken from them after a five-year court battle with real estate developers Oris and Mantis Van Sweringen. The Van Sweringens, who had built the Terminal Tower, the city's tallest building at the time, successfully attempted to take the brewery property by eminent domain so that the land could be cleared for the railroad approach to the main terminal. The entire brewery was razed in 1928. In the photograph above, the aging tanks are being removed from the stock house; in the photograph below, the brewery is about half-razed. The building at far right is the bottling plant, built in 1915. (Courtesy of the Cleveland State University Library, Cleveland Union Terminal Collection.)

By the early 1940s, the lingering effects of Prohibition could still be seen around Cleveland. Perhaps best representing the demise of the city's early breweries was the ruins of the once-thriving Cleveland Brewing Company on the city's far east side. Partially razed in 1938, the gutted brewhouse remained standing for another decade. According to a 1941 article in the *Cleveland Press*, visitors to the Brewery Restaurant, operating in a former saloon next door, often heard stories from former brewery wagon driver Jugend Blaett of ghosts in the upper floors that could be heard late at night, rolling barrels and pounding bungs in place. The viability of this claim was questioned only by the fact that Blaett could barely hear the interviewer's questions, having to cup his hand over his ear. Ghosts or not, the remaining buildings and stables were razed a few years later, leaving no remains at the site today. (Carl Miller collection.)

When Prohibition ended in April 1933, the Pilsener Brewing Company was the first in Cleveland to put its real beer back on the market. As it had continued to produce near beer throughout the era, it took little work to skip the de-alcoholization step from the brewing process. Even so, it was a full month later, on May 4, when the first P.O.C. Beer in 14 years was available for sale. The associated fuel and soft drink businesses were subsequently abandoned, as the beer business was immediately more profitable. This photograph shows some of Pilsener's wooden aging vats about to be put in use again. (Carl Miller collection.)

Four

REPEAL AND THE REBIRTH
OF THE INDUSTRY
1933–1984

Within three months of Pres. Franklin Roosevelt's inauguration, he had succeeded in having Congress modify the Volstead Act, allowing the sale of 3.2 percent beer. On April 7, 1933, beer appeared again in Ohio for the first time in nearly 14 years. By the end of the year, the 21st Amendment (often just referred to as Repeal) had been passed by Congress and ratified by 36 states, allowing the sale of full-strength beer and hard liquor as of December 5, 1933. The Prohibition era was officially over. At the old Leisy brewery, several months of rebuilding with all new equipment were followed by the first brew in the spring of 1934. Celebrating the return of Leisy's Beer are (from left to right) Herbert Leisy (grandson of Isaac), brewmaster Carl Faller, brewery employee Phillip Bernauer, and company officers Earle Johnson and Daniel Ford. (Bill Carlisle collection.)

THE MASH TUB

As the Leisy family had been out of the brewing business for some time, the plant had no brewing equipment and needed to start completely from scratch. New president Herbert F. Leisy was born in 1900 and was too young to be involved with the running of the company before Prohibition. However, at age 33 and with degrees from Yale University and the Harvard University School of Business, he was now in charge of the entire operation and oversaw the plant's resurrection, along with brewmaster Carl Faller, who had been with the company since 1900. Several views inside the renovated Leisy brewery appeared with a lengthy article in *Brewery Age* magazine in October 1934. The photograph to the left shows the mash tub, where the brewing process began; the photograph below shows the brew kettle, with Carl Faller standing nearby.

RICE COOKER AND MEAL SCALE HOPPER

Two more images of the Leisy brewing process, from *Brewery Age* magazine in 1934, appear here; the rice cooker is above, and the image below shows the end of the bottling line, with full bottles going into crates. Initially, the same three brands were available as before Prohibition: Leisy's Premium, Leisy's Special Brew, and Leisy's Extra Pale. A huge, planned celebration ensued when the finished products were first made available for sale on May 14. Local celebrities were present, and there were live radio broadcasts from the plant, as the festivities went on well into the night. The family's name had obviously been remembered by many Clevelanders—the plant's initial annual capacity was 120,000 barrels, but this was not nearly enough to supply the tremendous demand for Leisy's Beer. Later that summer, the capacity had risen to 240,000 barrels, and the company stated that it was the city's leader in beer sales once again.

BOTTLING STEP—LABELLING

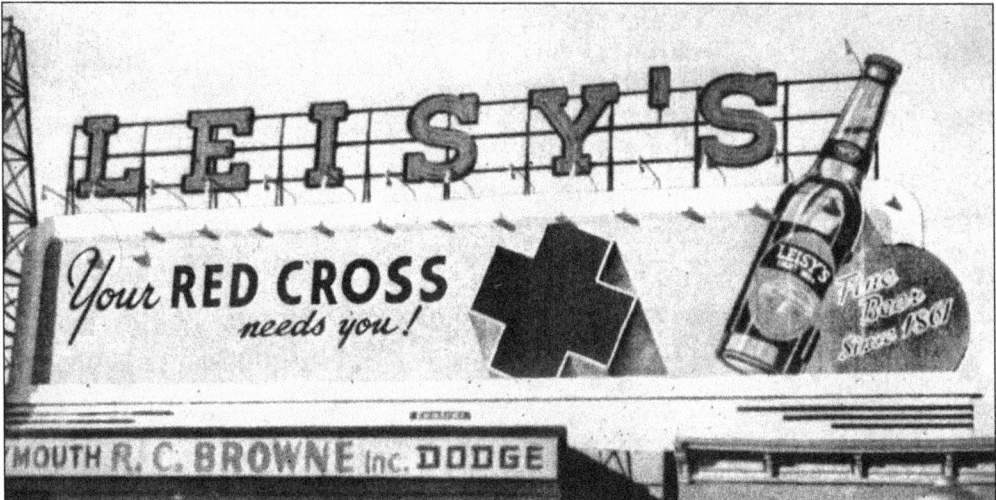

Leisy's Light Beer was introduced in 1940. Lighter in color and in body than the older, more traditional beers, the new style sold well and remains popular to this day. However, light beer in the sense of low calories did not start to appear in the city for many more years. This billboard, reflecting the early days of America's involvement in World War II, was reportedly seen by nearly 500,000 Clevelanders each day. (*Modern Brewery Age* trade magazine, February 1942.)

This cardboard sign was distributed to beverage store and bar owners in the 1940s, reminding their employees how to manage their stock of Leisy Beer. Selling the oldest bottled or kegged beer first, keeping the equipment clean, and assuring the proper function of all equipment was critical to keeping customers happy. One bad batch of beer, either having a poor taste or going flat, could cause a beer drinker to switch allegiance to another brand. (Bill Carlisle collection.)

The Great Lakes Exposition was held from June 27 to October 4, 1936, at a 135-acre site along the city's lakefront. The huge event stretched from Cleveland Municipal Stadium to East Twenty-second Street and was similar to a world's fair, with commercial exhibits, many entertainment acts, many different types of food, and, of course, beer. This postcard shows an overview of the exposition, with the Leisy pavilion shown in the middle of the Alpine Village section. Black Forest Beer from the Cleveland Home Brewing Company also had a small pavilion there.

Cleveland's Forest City Brewery incorporated soon after Repeal, with former Cuyahoga County commissioner Jack Harris as president. With $400,000 worth of improvements to the plant on Union Avenue, the company was selling beer in the city by early summer. Its primary brand was Waldorf (German for "forest village" or "forest city") Beer and Ale. The company produced a special type of Waldorf Lager Beer in bottles for the Great Lakes Exposition in the summer of 1936.

Along with the improvements in brewing technology after Repeal, there were also improvements in packaging and marketing beer. In 1935 came the first appearance of beer in metal cans, when the Forest City Brewery sold Waldorf Beer and Ale in flat-topped cans made by the American Can Company. Retailers were initially skeptical about the new containers, which had just recently been invented, but canned beer would continue to be sold by Forest City on a small level until the onset of World War II. Shown here is one of the first cans to be produced in Cleveland.

Cab Over Engine Fleet for Bottle Beer Delivery, Cleveland. Striking Example of Beauty in Beer Truck

This is a page from a Forest City Brewery promotional brochure, produced in 1935. It shows two different types of delivery trucks as well as a picture of a painted sign on a barn in the region. Sales of Waldorf Beer were excellent in 1934; the company later claimed that one-fourth of the beer sold in Cleveland that year was Waldorf. However, once the city's other breweries were back at full production, its sales slumped, and the company declared bankruptcy in 1939. Business limped along for five more years before the plant was sold in 1944 to the Brewing Corporation of America for production of Black Label Beer and Red Cap Ale.

Although brewing at the site ceased in 1948, the Forest City brewery is one of four Cleveland breweries still standing today (the others being Baehr, Union, and Eilert). After losing its ornate tower and roof peaks over the years, it looks like any other industrial building in the city, although, in 1976, it was listed in the National Register of Historic Places.

The former Excelsior brewery on Sackett Avenue returned to brewing in 1933, renamed the Eilert Brewing Company for brewmaster Henry Eilert. The company's King Kole brand of beer and ale sold well in the Cleveland area and represented a significant portion of the company's sales in the 1930s. In 1940, the company's name was changed to King's Brewery, Inc., to better reflect what had become the company's anchor brands. Despite this, the brewery closed its doors for good in 1941.

The Pilsener brewery's annual capacity by the mid-1930s was 175,000 barrels, only slightly more than it had been 30 years earlier. Inside the plant's bottling works, the bottling process was still somewhat labor-intensive in 1933. As sales improved over the following decade and production at the plant continued to increase, the bottling process became increasingly mechanized and efficient, at the expense of jobs. (Cleveland State University Library collection.)

The Pilsener Brewing Company had undertaken a $300,000 expansion of the brewery in 1914, including a large building facing Clark Avenue that held a new bottling plant capable of filling 5,000 bottles per hour, an assembly hall, a rathskeller that could seat 500 guests, and an adjacent garage that housed the company's 30 delivery vehicles. After this, the five-acre complex at the southwest corner of Clark Avenue and West Sixty-fifth Street became known as Pilsener Square. After the brewhouse burned and was razed in 1998, the bottling building remains the only structure of the complex still standing today.

Prior to the appearance of large beer distributors, scenes like this one were seen throughout the Cleveland area in the 1930s, as each brewery had its own fleet of trucks to deliver beer to homes, stores, and restaurants, sometimes one case at a time. This photograph of a P.O.C. Beer truck is from the archives of the Schaefer Truck Company.

Between 1947 and 1951, $5 million was spent increasing the Pilsener brewery's annual capacity to 400,000 barrels (later improvements would bring this total to 500,000 barrels). The investment paid off quickly—by 1949, the company was operating at near-capacity with sales of 360,000 barrels. The expansion included the installation of a canning line for the first time, and P.O.C. Beer was first sold in cap-sealed cans (shown here) in 1949. The brand was available in both cap-sealed and flat-topped cans at different times until 1952, when the cone-topped cans were phased out (in a trend seen throughout the country, as this type of can was nearly gone by 1960). Despite the convenience and disposability of cans, approximately three-fourths of P.O.C. Beer was still packaged in bottles.

This photograph was taken around 1940 and shows two beer billboards standing atop buildings in Cleveland's Playhouse Square district, at the intersection of Euclid Avenue and Huron Road; East Fourteenth Street comes in from the left. The Erin Brew sign at right stands in front of the Halle Brothers Department Store building. The Wyndham Hotel building stands at the site of the billboard today. At the left is a large P.O.C. Beer sign in the form of a clock with a pendulum. (Carl Miller collection.)

TAXPAID AT THE RATE
PRESCRIBED BY
INTERNAL REVENUE LAW.

DOES NOT CONTAIN MORE THAN
4 PERCENTUM OF ALCOHOL
BY VOLUME.

STRENGTH

TRADE THE STANDARD MARK

ERIN BREW
EHREN BRAU

CONTENTS
12 FLUID OZ.   THIS BEER BOTTLED AT THE BREWERY

PERMIT OHIO-U-623

THE STANDARD BREWING CO.
CLEVELAND, OHIO.

In keeping with the Irish background of the founders of the Standard Brewing Company, the company's anchor brand for more than 50 years was known as Erin Brew, which roughly translated to "beer of Ireland." So as to not alienate the brewery's German customers, the earliest labels also carried the name "Ehren Brau," which roughly translated to "honored beer." This bottle label dates to 1934 and also shows the company's early logo of an eagle and beer barrel.

After Repeal, the Standard Brewing Company quickly returned to the beer business. Although production of near beer had ceased several years earlier, the brewing equipment had remained intact, and in late May, Standard became the city's third brewery to release the real thing to the public. Under new brewmaster Gotthold Kuebler, the Erin Brew and Standard Old Bohemian brands quickly became Cleveland favorites again. In an attempt to take advantage of the initial rush for beer that spring, Standard had hired 150 new employees by the time that the beer was released, to help keep up with the demand. Crates of Erin Brew Beer are shown here being loaded from the brewery's loading dock into a delivery truck, soon after Repeal. (Carl Miller collection.)

Outdoor beer advertising took different forms in the 1940s, but two of the most commons forms were large billboards, often perched atop the roofs of large buildings in the city, and signs placed on trolleys and buses. In this image from the 1940s, the same advertisement for Erin Brew Beer appears in both forms at the same time.

This advertisement for the "Ranch Ten-O-Two" television program, featuring country music legend Pee Wee King, appeared in the *Plain Dealer* in March 1954. It was named after Formula Ten-O-Two, a new recipe and advertising campaign for the Erin Brew brand.

From Bottle House to Garage . . .

"It pays to modernize"

. . Reports George E. Creadon,
General Manager
Standard Brewing Company
Cleveland, Ohio

MODERN METHODS of beer delivery are as important in successful brewery operation as the most efficient bottle line operation, according to George E. Creadon, general manager of Standard Brewing Company, Cleveland.

From the time empty bottles arrive until automatic conveyors load tasty Erin Brew into the waiting fleet of modern White Trucks, Standard achieves new efficiency in ultra-modern materials handling.

For many years, Standard has depended on Whites for beer deliveries in the Cleveland area. Now, the handsome new White 3000 achieves a new degree of usefulness . . . efficiency . . . delivery economy. It provides new driver time and energy savings . . . new traffic advantages . . . that make it tomorrow's truck today.

Ask your White Representative how this new White is engineered for greater usefulness . . . lower delivery cost . . . in your business.

THE WHITE MOTOR COMPANY
Cleveland 1, Ohio, U. S. A.

White SUPER POWER 3000

FOR MORE THAN 50 YEARS THE GREATEST NAME IN TRUCKS

Tips its cab to service

Many of the delivery trucks used by Cleveland brewers were produced by the local White Motor Company. With origins as the White Sewing Machine Company, it produced its first steam-powered car in 1901 and entered the truck business just over a decade later. Later rising to become one of the country's largest truck producers, the White name was still being used on trucks until 1995. This advertisement from *Modern Brewery Age* magazine in January 1951 shows the brand-new Standard Brewing Company bottling plant.

After the end of Prohibition, the large Gund Brewing Company plant overlooking Lake Erie stood vacant. New owners refurbished the plant in 1933, and the Sunrise Brewing Company was born, producing Sunrise, Golden Dawn, and Old German beers and ales. As it had not produced any beer in more than 14 years, the brewery needed a total overhaul, but once the new equipment was installed, the plant's annual capacity reached 75,000 barrels (later improvements would bring that number to 120,000 barrels). In this view of the west side of the plant (taken from the November 15, 1933, issue of *Modern Brewery* magazine), the new cooling tower made of California redwood is seen on the roof. This tower was positioned to take advantage of the cool winds that blow off Lake Erie, which serve as a natural cooling medium.

The Sunrise Brewing Company used early delivery trucks like this one to transport barrels and crates of beer around town. The company was purchased in 1940 by reputed underworld figure Alfred "Big Al" Polizzi. Polizzi operated the company successfully until selling it to the Brewing Corporation of America in 1944 for $400,000, after which brewing operations at the site ceased.

76

This Sunrise Brewing Company delivery truck is decorated as a float in a local parade around 1935. Between the eight women in flight suits and the airplane on top, it would appear to have been a theme relating to Charles Lindbergh's transatlantic flight in 1927, connected with the local brewery workers' union. (Carl Miller collection.)

Sunrise and Golden Dawn Beer remained steady sellers through 1938, when Tip Top Beer and Cheerio Ale were introduced. Brewed according to an old Bohemian recipe from brewmaster Jaro "Jerry" Pavlik's family, the brands were successful enough that just one year later, the company's name was changed to the Tip Top Brewing Company. This photograph shows a large roadside billboard for the new brands, taken from the *Modern Brewer* trade magazine, June 1938.

On May 26, 1933—14 years to the day after statewide Prohibition took effect—the Cleveland Home Brewing Company was back in business by releasing its Clevelander Beer to the public (the brand had been brewed before Prohibition by the Gund Brewing Company). That brand as well as later brands Meister Brau and Black Forest all came out of this brew kettle inside the plant on the city's east side, shown here about 1935. (Cleveland State University Library collection.)

For the most part, sterilizing, filling, and capping bottles had become a quick and efficient process by the late 1930s. Bottled beer continued to gain popularity over the next several decades, both in returnable long-necked bottles and squat, disposable bottles. This scene inside the Cleveland Home Brewing Company dates to 1940. (Cleveland State University Library collection.)

Like the city's other breweries, the Cleveland Home Brewing Company had its own fleet of delivery trucks in the mid-1930s. The truck above was fancier and used for home deliveries of bottled beer in cases into some of the city's more affluent neighborhoods. The truck below, seen outside the plant's loading dock, was more utilitarian and used to transport full barrels to local bars. (Above, Carl Miller collection; below, Bill Carlisle collection.)

Alessandro "Sonny" DeMaioribus had begun working in the Cleveland Home brewery's office several years prior to Prohibition, and he continued there throughout the next 30 years, becoming the company's vice president, secretary, and general manager by 1939. Sonny was behind the introduction that year of Sonny's Premium Beer, a higher-priced brand using higher-quality ingredients than the usual beer brands. Though not one of the company's best sellers, the brand continued in production for many years. Sonny also was well known in local politics as a member of city council, serving two terms as council president, and as chairman of the Cuyahoga County Republican party. He remained in local politics until his death in 1968 at age 70. Here he is seen in the brewery's office in the 1940s. (Cleveland State University Library collection.)

After World War II, the Cleveland Home Brewing Company's success began to drop off quickly, marked by the deaths of longtime president Omar Mueller (son of Ernst Mueller, the company's president prior to Prohibition) in 1946 and longtime brewmaster George Lezius in 1947. Sonny DeMaioribus purchased the remaining stock in the company and appointed his brother, Dr. Anthony D. DeMaioribus, as the new brewmaster, the latter giving up his dental practice in the process. The decline in sales was due to a number of factors, including a dramatic increase in competition from national and regional breweries. Here Anthony DeMaioribus is seen inside the brewery's laboratory in the 1940s. (Cleveland State University Library collection.)

In October 1933 came what would become the Cleveland Home Brewing Company's flagship brand for the next 18 years, Black Forest Beer, which supposedly was brewed from an 11th-century Bavarian recipe. It was brewed under the supervision of brewmaster George Lezius, a veteran of the Cleveland brewing industry. Shown here is a bottle label for the brand; the name resurfaced in 1994, when it was used for several years as a brand of beer made by the Crooked River Brewing Company in the Flats.

Post-Prohibition improvements in the Cleveland Home brewery had increased the plant's annual capacity to 175,000 barrels, although the company's peak production was only 111,000 barrels in 1945. This had dwindled to 35,000 barrels in 1951, despite the addition of a new brand, Dee Light Beer and Ale, and the addition of a canning line for the packaging of Black Forest and Dee Light Beers in cap-sealed cans. Seeing no improvements ahead, the company stopped beer production in January 1952, and the equipment was auctioned off. This photograph shows a large rooftop billboard for the new but short-lived brand in early 1951. (Bill Carlisle collection.)

This image from *Brewery Age* magazine in September 1934 shows a view inside the Fishel–Cleveland and Sandusky brewery's power plant and the machinery that ran the refrigeration equipment. Advances in refrigeration technology over the previous 20 years were a major factor in the rapid growth of the brewing industry after Repeal. No longer dependent on ice, breweries were now able to transport beer much farther to new markets.

The old Fishel–Cleveland and Sandusky brewery on East Fifty-fifth Street was refurbished in 1933, and subsequent brewing operations were overseen by brewmaster John Aubele Jr., although after his death in 1935, he was succeeded by Frank Gollwitzer and Charles Neumann. With the plant's modernization, its annual capacity reached 120,000 barrels, a number that would increase to 200,000 barrels in later years. In this image from *Brewery Age* magazine in September 1934, "the Voice in the Sky" airplane uses an amplifier to announce Gold Bond Beer messages to Clevelanders.

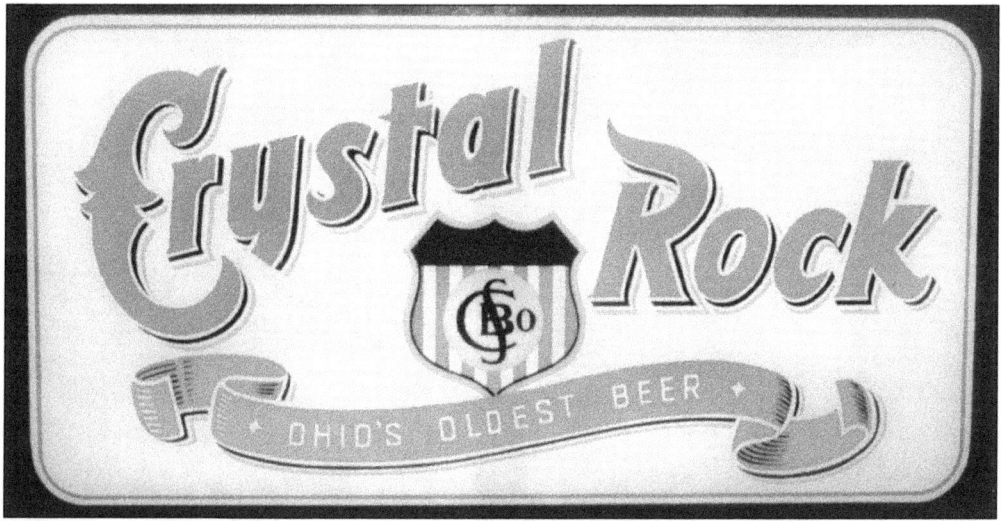

Crystal Rock Beer was one of the mainstays of the Cleveland and Sandusky Brewing Company throughout its existence. First brewed in 1893 by the Stang brewery in Sandusky, it was named after the Crystal Rock spring from which the water for brewing was taken. Although the Stang brewery survived Prohibition, it closed in 1935, leaving the plant on East Fifty-fifth Street in Cleveland as the sole brewery in the company. The Crystal Rock brand was produced there until 1962, when the plant closed, after which it was brewed in other cities for several years. This is a painted glass sign from the 1940s.

Old Timers Ale was a new brand for Cleveland and Sandusky after Repeal. Some of its early advertising connected with the company's history, stating "Brewed by Old Timers/Since '98," when the company was first formed. One of few ales brewed in Cleveland after Prohibition, the brand remained popular until the brewery closed in 1962, after which it continued to be produced at breweries in Findlay and Toledo, Ohio, as well as in Buffalo, New York, and Cumberland, Maryland, into the late 1960s.

Gold Bond Beer was originally brewed in 1905 and remained the Cleveland and Sandusky's flagship brand after Repeal. This photograph shows a delivery truck (made by Cleveland's White Motor Company) outside the brewery's loading dock in 1949. The company's original fleet of 25 GM trucks grew considerably over the years, delivering beer throughout northeast Ohio.

Beer advertising continued to take more unique forms after Repeal. This painted plaster statue of a bartender serving Gold Bond Beer was used in the 1940s; a nearly identical statue exists for Crystal Rock Beer. This type of statue is also known as a "chalk" sign, although it is not actually made of chalk. (Glenn Kuebeler collection.)

The president of the
Cleveland-Sandusky Brewing
Corporation (previously Cleveland
and Sandusky before Prohibition) after
1949 was Homer Marshman, a local
attorney and businessman. Marshman
was already known to Clevelanders as
one of the founders of the Cleveland
Rams NFL football team in 1936,
and although the team had moved
to Los Angeles in 1946, Marshman
became one of the owners of the newer
Cleveland Browns NFL franchise in
1954. In the mid–1950s, the company
began sponsoring Cleveland Browns
television broadcasts, largely through
Marshman's connection with the team.
This is a Browns game program from
November 20, 1955; note the references
to the Browns' NFL championship from
the previous season.

Radio and television were quickly becoming integral parts of American culture in the late 1940s
and early 1950s. Taking advantage of this, the Standard Brewing Company sponsored various
programs on both radio and television, but the biggest coup was the company's sponsorship of
the 1948 Cleveland Indians radio broadcasts. Cleveland has always been known for its sports
fans, and the fans listened to the radio in record numbers that year when the Indians won the
American League pennant and eventually the World Series. This propelled Erin Brew Beer to
be the top seller in the city until 1951. The power of mass media was just beginning to be tapped.
Here Jimmy Dudley, the radio voice of the Indians for 20 years, poses with his sponsor.

BREWERS EVERYWHERE REPORT . . .

"THIS GREAT NEW WHITE IS SAVING TIME...CUTTING OUR DELIVERY COSTS"

ITS usefulness can't be matched . . . its efficiency sets a new standard for beer deliveries . . . its economy substantially reduces truck operating costs.

It's the entirely *new* White 3000 for the specialized needs of brewers everywhere. "The design of the White 3000," reports Herbert F. Leisy, president of Leisy Brewing Company, Cleveland, "provides greater payload within legal limits, and that's easy on the pocketbook. It means at least an extra 50 cases on each trip."

Leisy driver-salesmen who drive the Whites, garage maintenance men, and management interested in economical performance all report this new White is ideal for their delivery service.

In every way, this truck of tomorrow, is engineered for the exacting needs of the industry. Ask your White Representative for the facts about this entirely new truck that saves time and reduces truck costs . . . because it's *miles* ahead!

LOOK HOW IT SAVES!

drivers like its maneuverability . . . save time in every phase of delivery.

operators get more goods delivered in less time for reduced delivery cost.

mechanics do better work . . . quicker because of complete front-end accessibility . . . instantly.

THE WHITE MOTOR COMPANY
Cleveland 1, Ohio, U. S. A.
THE WHITE MOTOR COMPANY OF CANADA LIMITED • FACTORY AT MONTREAL

White
SUPER POWER
3000

Tips its cab to service

FOR MORE THAN 50 YEARS THE GREATEST NAME IN TRUCKS

This advertisement in *Modern Brewery Age* magazine from February 1950 shows one of a fleet of 36 Leisy Brewing Company delivery trucks from the local White Motor Company. This fleet was part of the $1.5 million spent on plant improvements after World War II, which also included a new modern bottling complex that remains standing today on Vega Avenue.

Here are two images of local delivery trucks, made by the International Harvester Company, for the Leisy Brewing Company, taken from *Modern Brewer* magazine in February 1936. Most of the trucks (like the one above) were designed for the transporting, loading, and unloading of kegs, but the van shown below was specifically used for home and restaurant deliveries of bottle crates and four-gallon growlers (large cans that were similar to party kegs that are made today; they required the use of a bicycle pump to build internal pressure for tapping the beer).

This is one of many trolley cars that carried beer advertising in the city, and it shows the new logo that Leisy unveiled in the early 1950s. Near the top of the city's beer sales prior to World War II, the company had lost that position by 1948, as the Erin Brew and P.O.C. brands skyrocketed in sales with large postwar expansions and slick marketing campaigns. Although Leisy remained a popular brand in Cleveland, its sales gradually declined as national and other local brands continued to slowly gain larger shares of the local market. Sales dropped from over 330,000 barrels in 1949 to less than 150,000 barrels by 1955.

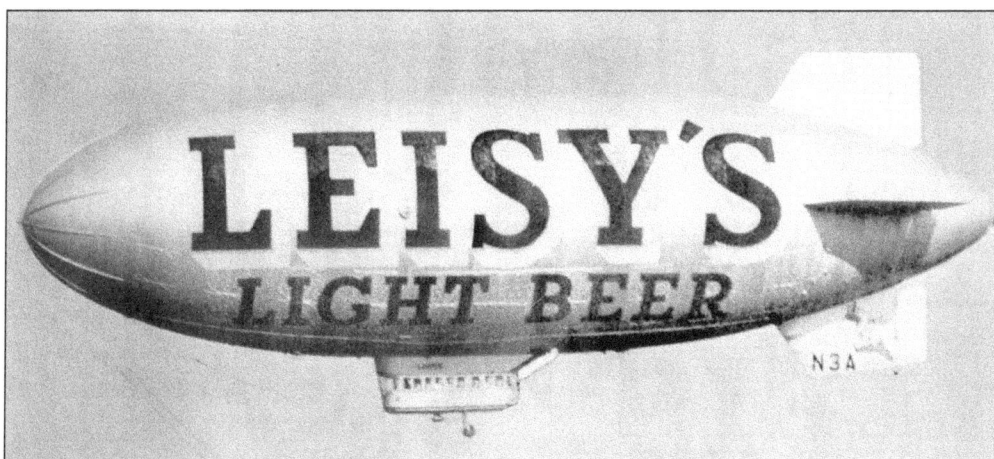

By the 1950s, advertising had begun to take on more varied and creative forms. For several months in the summer of 1950, the Leisy Brewing Company rented this 154-foot-long blimp, formerly used during World War II for patrolling the nation's coasts, for advertising its beer. Stationed in nearby Akron, the blimp flew all across northern Ohio, visiting cities where Leisy had distributors.

On the other hand, Leisy's horse-drawn beer wagons evoked a sense of nostalgia and were used for local promotional activities in the 1950s. This image is from a postcard used to send information to distributors and potential Leisy customers.

It's Here!

LEISY'S
90th Anniversary Beer

The year 1952 marked the Leisy family's 90th year in the brewing business, and this fact was celebrated throughout the year, along with a celebration of the company's 300 millionth gallon of beer produced. In the same year came the repackaging of Leisy's Light Beer, a brand which had already been around for more than a decade, targeted at the increasing number of consumers who were seeking a beer with lighter body than the older brands. The anniversary year was the company's last profitable one, after which came a seven-year slide into oblivion. This is a cardboard bus sign from the anniversary year. (Bill Carlisle collection.)

Much of the Standard brewery on Train Avenue was built in 1906–1907, although large additions to the plant were built in the 1940s. In 1948, a two-year expansion project began, costing $4.5 million. Consisting of a new four-story brew house and stock house, and a large modern bottling facility at the west end of the complex, the expansion increased the plant's annual capacity to 550,000 barrels, making it the city's second-largest brewery. Taken by brewery employee Ed Kintop, this view of the plant is looking east on Train Avenue in the 1950s.

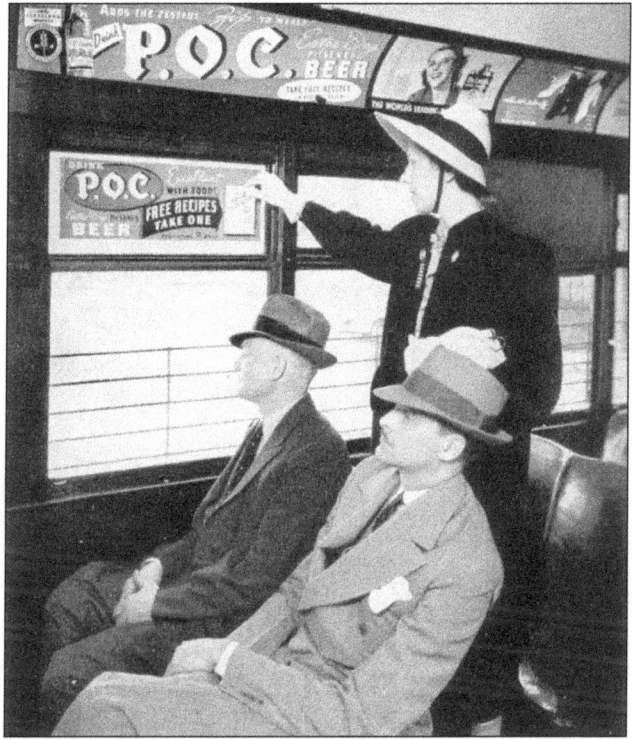

This Pilsener Brewing Company advertising campaign for P.O.C. Beer was highlighted in the November 1939 issue of *Brewery Age* magazine. In the photograph to the right, recipe booklets were given out on streetcars in cooperation with the United Brewers Industrial Foundation. Recipe books for foods that went with beer or that used beer in the recipe were inexpensive giveaways that many different brewers used during the era. In the photograph below, the top sign was a generic one for beer, while the bottom sign used a mirror to get the rider's attention.

In addition to P.O.C. Beer, the Pilsener Brewing Company also had Toby Ale (named after an English folklore character), which hit the market in 1940. Brewed as a true top-fermented ale, with higher-quality ingredients and selling at a higher price, the brand remained available through the early 1950s, although it never caught on in a big way with local beer drinkers. This image shows a painted tin sign for the brand from the early 1940s. (Ken Bryson collection.)

Pilsener Pete was a generic character dressed in a traditional Bavarian outfit that frequently appeared in P.O.C.'s advertisements in the early 1950s, such as the cardboard bus sign seen here. Despite the company's claim that the new "Genuine 51 Flavor" was based on the brand's original recipe from 50 years earlier, it was actually more consistent with the current national trend toward light-bodied, less-filling beers. The Genuine 51 Flavor campaign was a resounding success—within two years of its appearance, the company's sales had doubled, and P.O.C. had become the city's sales leader, a position where it would remain for several years.

The Standard brewery's new bottling facility opened in March 1950. The huge three-story facility featured state-of-the-art equipment that allowed the company to can its beer for the first time, utilizing flat-topped steel cans, 210 of which could be filled per minute by the new equipment. Some of the modern bottle filling equipment, as seen below, was photographed some years later by brewery employee Ed Kintop. Although the brewery closed in 1971, the bottling building remains standing today, housing a U-Haul truck depot, and is easily visible from Interstate 90. (Above, Carl Miller collection.)

The Standard brewery was purchased in 1961 by the F&M Schaefer Brewing Company of New York City. Already well established on the East Coast, the company was attempting to expand its markets to the west. Despite an investment of $1.5 million to upgrade the plant, Schaefer sold the brewery three years later to the C. Schmidt Brewing Company of Philadelphia. This photograph was taken by employee Ed Kintop at the time of the transition from Standard to Schaefer in 1961.

After Schmidt's purchase of the brewery in 1964, it continued to operate the plant successfully for another seven years. Improvements had raised its annual capacity to 700,000 barrels, but in 1971, Schmidt was looking to increase its production further and purchased the recently closed Carling brewery on the city's east side. After that, the Train Avenue plant was purchased by the Miller Brewing Company of Milwaukee, which removed all brewing equipment and sent it to the Miller plant in Fort Worth, Texas. The nearly 70-year-old plant stood empty for a time before being razed in 1974. (Cleveland State University Library collection.)

At 33, James Alvin Bohannon was one of the country's youngest chief executives of a major corporation when, in 1929, he joined Cleveland's Peerless Motor Car Corporation, which was beginning to struggle at the outset of the Great Depression. Two years later, the decision was made to stop automobile production altogether and convert the huge automobile factory at East Ninety-third Street and Quincy Avenue into a brewery. In 1934, the new plant opened as the Brewing Corporation of America, the city's largest brewery ever.

The Brewing Corporation of America was the city's only major brewery to start from scratch after the end of Prohibition. The Peerless Corporation's president, James A. Bohannon, made connections with Canada's well-established Carling Brewing Company, and soon the huge factory was converted into a brewery for the production of the two main Carling brands: Black Label Beer and Red Cap Ale. This photograph shows one of many trucks in the area used to transport the new brands.

THE CLEVELAND PLANT

This is an artist's rendering of the Brewing Corporation of America plant on Quincy Avenue, along with company president James A. Bohannon, taken from a company brochure in 1946. The rear sections represented the original Peerless automobile factory, completed in 1909, although this section of the plant was later razed and replaced with modern structures that held many of the aging tanks for beer, as the company grew and its annual capacity eventually reached 3 million barrels. The front portion of the plant, facing Quincy Avenue, originally held Peerless corporate offices and design labs, and upon conversion to a brewery, the eastern wing (shown with steam coming out of the top) was enlarged to five stories to house the new brew house. The brewery finally closed in 1984, and the plant was completely razed a decade later, leaving an empty lot at the site today.

Upon the opening of the new Brewing Corporation of America plant in 1934, the public was invited inside to see the transformation. Here the two large brew kettles stand inside the new marble-lined, art deco-style brew house, a very unusual appearance for an industrial setting such as a brewery. The windows looked right out onto Quincy Avenue so that passersby could see the kettles inside.

As the brewing process progressed, the liquid from the brew kettle (called wort) passed into these huge cypress fermentation tanks, as seen in this view from *Brewery Age* magazine, July 1938.

Most of the fermenting tanks were open at the top to allow for release of gas from the fermentation process. Some breweries would maintain their own secret strains of yeast to give their beers a specific flavor. These tanks are shown in 1945. (Cleveland State University Library collection.)

Cellars with rows of glass-lined steel storage tanks filled much of the rear portion of the Brewing Corporation of America plant, as shown in *Brewery Age* magazine, July 1938. After fermentation was completed, the liquid would go into these tanks to age for several weeks before it could be truly called beer.

The bottling department of the Brewing Corporation of America was filled with huge, state-of-the-art machines, made to handle the large volume of beer and ale being produced. This view from *Modern Brewer* magazine in 1938 shows one of four bottle soaker/cleaners in the new plant.

James A. Bohannon believed that the country's beer drinkers were ready for exclusively disposable packages in the 1930s. Disposable bottles and cans helped to reduce costs normally associated with shipping returnable bottles back to the brewery, especially from long distances. However, they had not yet achieved the widespread popularity of long-necked returnable bottles, which had been around since the late 19th century. In addition, draft beer in taverns remained as popular as it had been for many years. Therefore, when quart bottles disappeared in 1943, draft beer was discontinued in November 1944, and long-necked bottles were phased out in 1945, it was a roadblock to the successful marketing of Carling beers. Realizing this some time later, the company brought back all three forms of packaging. This image shows the nine large bottle filling machines in the bottling department.

This bottling line filled quart bottles at the Brewing Corporation of America plant in the 1950s. While 12-ounce bottles were always the standard size, there was always a loyal market for the larger-sized packages. (Cleveland State University Library collection.)

This image from the *Brewers Journal* in 1934 shows the racking room, where stainless steel barrels were filled for shipment of draft beer to taverns. By the late 1930s, however, the Brewing Corporation of America had taken a different strategy than most other brewers and was packaging 95 percent of its beer in bottles.

After a World War II-era restriction of metal use was lifted, Carling beer and ale appeared domestically in both 12- and 32-ounce cone-topped cans. Their appearance was not widespread, however, as the plant operated nine bottling lines to just one canning line. In this photograph from 1942, Mike Mahlenko works on the canning line, which had a capacity of 153,600 cans per 16-hour day. (Cleveland State University Library)

Red Cap Ale, originally brewed in Canada, was the brand chosen to be the anchor for the Brewing Corporation of America in 1934. While its sales never soared and it lingered in the shadow of the more popular Black Label brand of beer, it continued to have respectable sales throughout its 37 years of production in Cleveland. In 1944, the brand was the company's first to appear in metal cans, when these cap-sealed, cone-topped containers with camouflage-colored paint were made to be sent to troops fighting overseas in World War II.

This Carling Beer and Ale truck is from the 1930s and was primarily used for transport of beer in the greater Cleveland area. Overall, however, sales in the home region were not a high priority for the company, as its goal from the beginning was sales of Carling products nationwide. In the 1930s and 1940s, this was a huge challenge, and the costs of attempting to establish a national sales network nearly threw the company into bankruptcy. (Carl Miller collection.)

This delivery truck is from the 1950s and coincides with the change in the brewery's name in 1954 to the Carling Brewing Company, along with a complete overhaul of the logo and colors for the Black Label brand. By this time, the company had realized that its goal of making Red Cap Ale a successful anchor brand was not going to happen, while Black Label's sales continued to rise throughout the 1950s and early 1960s.

By the early 1950s, Carling had abandoned the use of the cap-sealed, cone-topped cans in favor of the flat-topped cans shown on the canning line here, inside the packaging building. The flat-topped cans were easier to store and stack in stores, making them far more popular with retailers. Despite this, bottled beer still remained more popular overall; even by the mid-1950s, the plant operated 10 bottling lines but only two canning lines. This photograph from the mid-1950s also shows the newly designed label for the Black Label brand. (Cleveland State University Library collection.)

Ian R. Dowie was the vice president of sales for Canadian Breweries, Ltd., which was the parent company that essentially owned Cleveland's Brewing Corporation of America. Dowie was transferred to Cleveland in 1948 to help bring the American company back from the brink of bankruptcy, and in 1951, he became president of the company. His shrewd marketing abilities helped catapult the company from 62nd in national sales in 1949 to 8th in 1957. He returned to Canada in 1962 to continue managing the Canadian company. (Carl Miller collection.)

This view shows the Carling brewery laboratory, as seen in *Brewery Age* magazine, July 1938. The science of brewing had become highly advanced by that time, and a trained brewmaster also needed to be a chemist and biologist, with knowledge of different strains of yeast, as well as different types of hops, barley, and so forth and knowledge of all the different chemical reactions that took place in the brewing process.

The barn motif was used in the early 1960s and included several different paper and cardboard point-of-sale items, to be used in supermarkets and beverage stores. The dancers in the barn bounced back and forth when a battery was placed underneath, while the six-pack carriers themselves were shaped like barns. This sort of packaging was more expensive than the simple piece of plastic that holds six-packs together today, but it was an effective tool for getting the buyer's attention. (Photographs of cardboard point-of-sale signs, Carl Miller collection.)

Stand-up signs such as this were commonly seen in grocery stores and beverage stores in the 1960s. This particular one mentions the "Mabel . . . Black Label" slogan that first appeared in Carling advertising in 1949 and continued to appear in the vast majority of Black Label advertising through the mid-1960s. To this day, it is still remembered by many people who watched television or listened to radio during the era, as the phrase was heard often. On television, Mabel was played by actress Jeanne Goodspeed, who brought out Black Label Beer before giving a trademark wink to the camera. The phrase was one of the earliest and certainly most successful national marketing campaigns for a brand of beer.

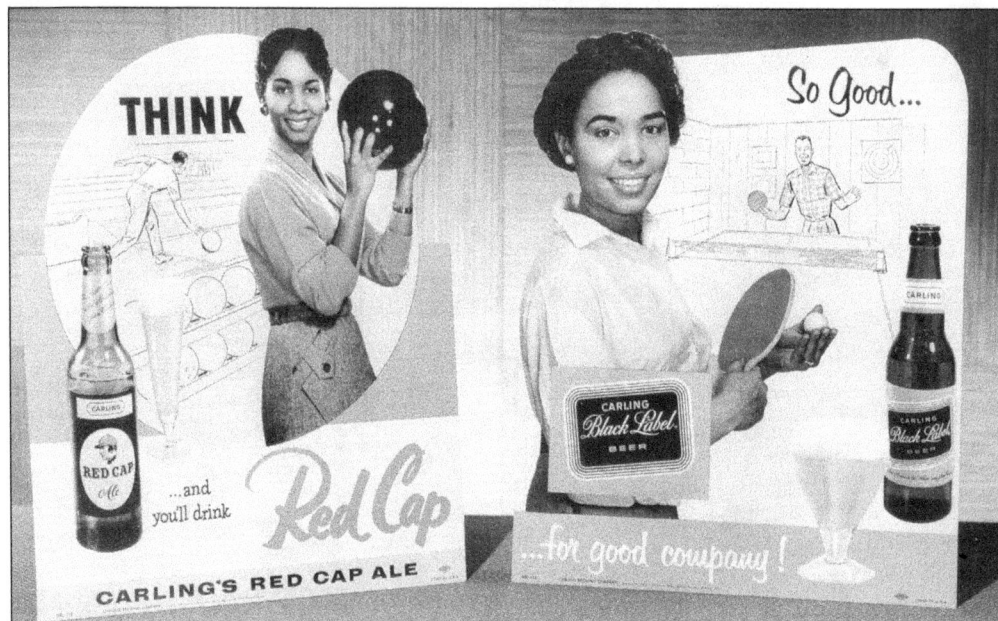

Traditionally, virtually all beer advertising was aimed at men. By the mid-1950s, however, many brewers had begun to target their advertising at women and minorities, a process known as market segmentation. (Still photographs of cardboard point-of-sale signs, Carl Miller collection.)

In its first 15 years of business, Carling chose not to market its products more heavily in Cleveland than in other cities. By the mid-1950s, however, Carling management had realized the value of marketing its products heavily in its home city, and sponsorship of the Cleveland Browns, Indians, and Barons broadcasts eventually followed, continuing throughout the 1960s. By this time, most of the city's other brewers, which had previously sponsored the local teams, had closed their doors. (Still photographs of cardboard point-of-sale signs, Carl Miller collection.)

All of Carling's products, in all available package types and sizes, including the very short-lived Carling Malt Liquor and Black Label Draft brands, are shown in a promotional brochure from around 1965. The company operated nine breweries from coast to coast at the time and had recently peaked at 5.7 million barrels in annual sales, as it placed at fourth nationally, behind only Anheuser-Busch, Schlitz, and Falstaff. The company's fortunes would soon turn sour, however. (Bill Carlisle collection.)

The latter half of the 1960s saw Carling's sales slowly decrease for a variety of reasons, as it dropped to eighth in national sales. Drastic measures were needed to keep the company profitable, and the apparent answer was to cut overhead by getting rid of the excessive brewing capacity in the company. The Cleveland plant was the oldest in the group, and while it was not necessarily as outdated as Carling subsequently claimed, it was chosen to be the first one closed. On May 9, 1971, when brewing ceased at the plant, it came as a great shock to the community, as more than 600 jobs were lost or transferred, including management. Brewer Jack Gabrenya, pictured here, was one of those who was set to lose his job. (Cleveland State University Library collection.)

Despite Carling's abandonment of its Cleveland plant, it was not the end of brewing at the site. The C. Schmidt Brewing Company was still operating at the old Standard plant on the city's west side, and once the Carling plant closed, Schmidt saw it as an opportunity to expand its operations. With an annual capacity of 3 million barrels, the Quincy Avenue plant quadrupled Schmidt's potential output in Cleveland. By early 1972, Schmidt had relocated to the city's east side and continued operations there for another 12 years. The entrance to the plant, seen here, remained an impressive sight in the 1970s. (Carl Miller collection.)

Once Schmidt had committed itself to keeping the Quincy Avenue brewery operating, it had the support of the local brewery workers' union. Anthony Sapienza, union president, recognized the importance of supporting the city's last remaining brewery, and he launched a campaign by the union to encourage local establishments to carry Schmidt's Beer. He also suggested that the city give the brewery a break on its substantial water and sewer bill, although no break was ever given. This is a jacket patch for the local teamsters' union.

P.O.C.
half time...
any time.

P.O.C.
PILSENER ON CALL

Pilsener Brewing Co., Cleveland, Ohio.

In 1972, Schmidt acquired the rights to brew the brands of the recently closed Duquesne Brewing Company of Pittsburgh. Duquesne had always maintained a healthy following in Ohio, and it had continued to brew the local favorite P.O.C. brand since the closing of Cleveland's Pilsener Brewing Company in 1962. These brands were packaged under the name of the original company, so P.O.C. labels still stated Pilsener Brewing Company. The brand finally disappeared from the market in 1987, after the Schmidt breweries in Cleveland and Philadelphia had closed. This advertisement is from a Cleveland Browns souvenir program in 1973.

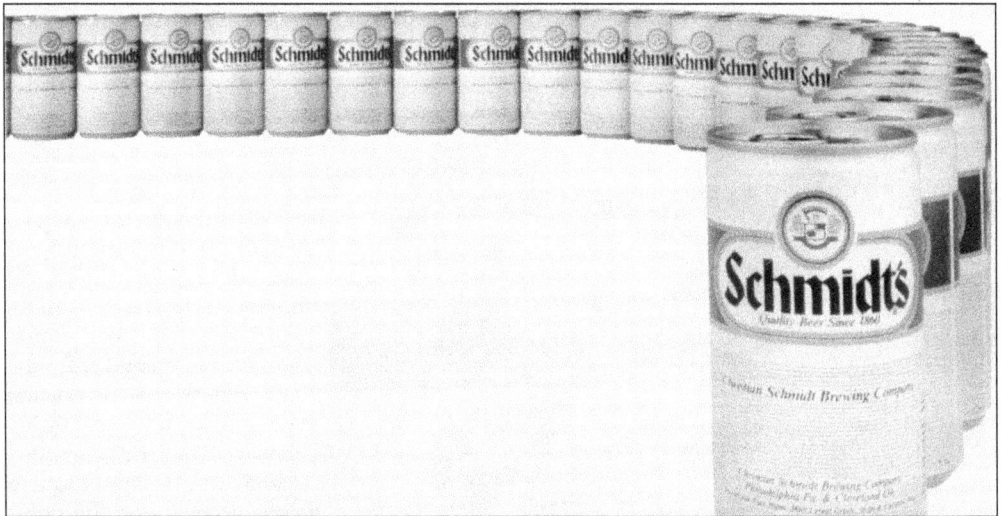

In 1981, the company redesigned its labels and renamed itself as the Christian Schmidt Brewing Company. By this time, however, the company had begun to see dwindling sales, as competition from the larger national companies continued to take a toll and the costs of operation continued to grow. This trend only worsened over the next three years, and in June 1984, the decision was made to close the Cleveland plant for good. When the last Schmidt's Beer rolled off the line that year, it marked the end of 150-plus years of brewing beer in the Forest City. But not for long . . .

110

Five

THE MODERN ERA
1988–PRESENT

In 1988, the city's brewing industry was reborn with the founding of the Great Lakes Brewing Company, the state's first brewpub. Located at 2516 Market Avenue in the Ohio City district on the near west side of Cleveland, the company was the brainchild of brothers Patrick and Daniel Conway. The new venture occupied structures originally built in 1864 and which had previously housed the Market Tavern and McClean's Feed and Seed. Its centerpiece is a huge, mahogany bar, thought to be the city's oldest. Eliot Ness, the real-life leader of "the Untouchables," had frequented the same bar many years earlier, when he had become the city's safety director, years after taking down Al Capone and his gang.

The Great Lakes brewpub stands just one block away from Cleveland's famed West Side Market on West Twenty-fifth Street, which operates to this day. In addition, it stands about midway between the sites of the large Schlather and Gehring breweries of the city's pre-Prohibition era. Historically, the site was ideal for a Cleveland-oriented brewing establishment.

Great Lakes eventually grew to become a full microbrewery, with new brewing and bottling facilities built in 1997 in the former Schlather Brewing Company stables and bottling works across the street. Costing in the neighborhood of $7 million, this expansion included a 75-barrel brewing system and elevated the plant's annual capacity to 70,000 barrels. In 2002, the brewery sold over 21,000 barrels (an impressive 17 percent increase over 2001), making it the country's 52nd-largest brewer, and this number continued to rise in the following years as the Great Lakes brands were being distributed throughout the Great Lakes region, as far west as Chicago and as far east as Washington, D.C.

Several stainless steel brew kettles are seen inside the brewhouse, where all brewing operations are controlled by computer. The company maintains an on-site process control lab, in which the brewers sample various brews each morning for quality of aroma, appearance, and taste. The beer is sampled at all stages of production and during shelf life. In addition, all equipment is swabbed to check for harmful bacteria. (Great Lakes Brewing Company.)

The Great Lakes bottling works is on the first floor of the brewery; the company uses only brown bottles with tall cardboard carriers to minimize the amount of light that can penetrate to the beer. Ultraviolet rays in light speed the breakdown of beer and the subsequent destruction of taste. (Great Lakes Brewing Company.)

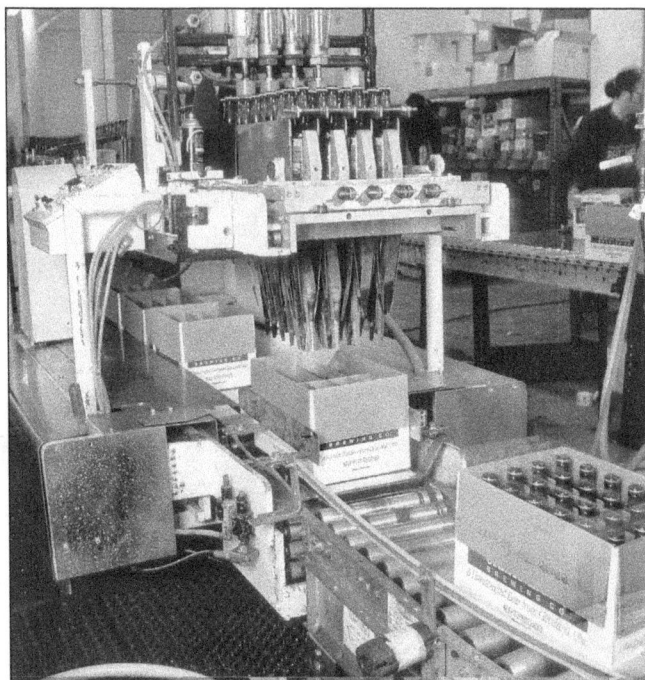

This is a view of the end of the bottling line, where the bottles are placed into cartons of either 6 or 24. Prior to being packed, the bottles pass through a device that seals the bottles by forcing oxygen out of them with carbon dioxide, helping to ensure freshness for a longer period. Even a tiny amount of oxygen left in the bottle can allow the process of oxidation to occur, which can destroy the beer's taste. This is critical for a craft brewer, who does not move product off the shelves as quickly as a large national brewery. (Great Lakes Brewing Company)

GREAT LAKES
BREWING CO.

Locktender Lager

GOVERNMENT WARNING: (1) ACCORDING TO THE SURGEON GENERAL, WOMEN SH
NOT DRINK ALCOHOLIC BEVERAGES DURING PREGNANCY BECAUSE OF THE RISK O
DEFECTS. (2) CONSUMPTION OF ALCOHOLIC BEVERAGES IMPAIRS YOUR ABILITY T
A CAR OR OPERATE MACHINERY, AND MAY CAUSE HEALTH PROBLEMS

A Munich style lager that is lighter in body with a sunny golden hue and soft malty finish. Named after the 19th Century fellows who tended the locks along the Ohio & Erie canal and also tended bar at their inns servicing many a thirsty traveler.

In keeping with the Bavarian Purity Law of 1516, this beer is traditionally brewed from all-natural ingredients: barley, hops, yeast and water. No chemicals or preservatives are used. Alcohol content by weight 3.9%; by volume 4.8%.

CA redemption. Refund ME, VT, CT, DE, MA, NY, IA, OR 5¢, MI 10¢.

Brewed & bottled by:
Great Lakes® Brewing Co.
2516 Market Avenue
Cleveland, OH 44113
(216) 771-4404
www.greatlakesbrewing.com

For freshest taste, please enjoy by:

Great Lakes has bottled more than 20 different brands of beer and ale over its first 17 years of business. Dortmunder Gold has been the best selling and has won numerous national awards; most other brands have had some sort of local historical or cultural connections associated with them, such as Burning River Pale Ale, the Eliot Ness Amber Lager Beer, the Edmund Fitzgerald Porter, Conway's Irish Ale, the Holy Moses White Ale, Commodore Perry India Pale Ale, Moondog Ale, Cleveland Brown Ale, and a newer brand shown here, Locktender Lager (named for the nearby Ohio Canal, the locktenders of which also served as tavern owners during the early 19th century).

The first brewing operation in the historic Flats district in nearly a century, the Crooked River Brewing Company opened its doors in June 1994 as the city's first true microbrewery. Operating in the former Scottish Tool and Die Building at 1101 Center Street, across the street from the Center Street bridge that spans the Cuyahoga River (the only operating swing bridge in the country), the brewery incorporated its location into its image and marketing from the beginning. In fact, the brewery's name was most fitting, as "Cuyahoga" is the Mohawk tribe name for "crooked river."

Aggressive marketing in the company's early years had Crooked River Beer available at over 1,000 outlets in northeast Ohio by 1997. Sales grew from 3,300 barrels in 1995 (the first full year in business) to around 9,000 barrels in 1998. Initially the beer was transported by the company itself instead of by outside distributors; shown here is one of the brewery's delivery trucks outside the brewery's loading dock, in the shadow of the Detroit-Superior High Level Bridge.

In the summer of 1997, the Crooked River Brewing Company was one of the primary sponsors of the Medic Drug Cleveland Grand Prix at Burke Lakefront Airport downtown. Intense marketing (as well as expansion of the brewery) sold a lot of beer, but it came at a heavy price. As the company was growing very rapidly, it required significant investment from outside sources to pay for new equipment and expensive marketing agreements. By 1998, financial problems led to a reorganization of the company's management, leading to the eventual purchase of the brewery by local entrepreneur C. David Snyder. By the end of 2000, however, the brewery had closed its doors.

Costing $1.5 million to construct, the Crooked River brewery began operation with an annual capacity of 6,000 barrels, although within three years, additional improvements had doubled this number. Brewmaster Stephen Danckers created the recipes for all of the beers produced by the company; among them were Black Forest Lager (taking the name from the popular brand made until the 1950s by the Cleveland Home Brewing Company), Settlers Ale, Lighthouse Gold (a bottle label of which is shown here), Bicentennial Beer (for the city's bicentennial in 1996), Island Hops, Erie Nights Pumpkin Brew, and Cool Mule Porter.

In 1999, Crooked River released Expansion Draft, a Kolsch-style ale that was made to celebrate the return of the new expansion Cleveland Browns football team to the NFL in that year. As soon as the team began playing in its new lakefront stadium, the brewery also began making Stadium Lager to sell during Browns games. In an unusual twist in the microbrewery industry, the brand was packaged in 16-ounce aluminum cans.

The Diamondback Brewery and Pub opened in 1996 on Prospect Avenue in the city's Gateway district and offered three levels of dining and entertainment along with a 15-barrel brewery. The pub saw rapid success, especially on days when the Indians or Cavaliers were playing, and the new venture was voted the "Best New Restaurant for 1997" by *Cleveland Magazine*. Despite the popularity of Diamondback, its success still depended largely on sporting events. While the Indians had tremendous success in the late 1990s, which led to hundreds of sold-out games a half mile from the brewpub, this only represented six months of the year. The relatively dismal performance of the Cavaliers during this same period led to decreasing attendance at Gund Arena. Despite several menu changes, the popular spot closed in early 2000. A later attempt to operate the site as Barons Brewpub lasted for only three months.

The Powerhouse, in the Flats district of the city, is a century-old structure known for its two huge smokestacks, and it was originally used to generate power for the city's electric railway and streetcar system. For many years, it had sat vacant, vandalized, and awaiting the wrecker's ball, until the district was renovated in the early 1990s. A cornerstone of the building's renovation was the opening in 1995 of the Rock Bottom Brewery and Restaurant, which was one in a chain of similar brewpubs across the country. Serving an array of locally themed beers, such as Terminal Stout, Riverbend Red Ale, Powerhouse Pale Ale, Walleye Wheat Beer, and Dawg Pound Brown Ale (after a nickname for the Cleveland Browns football team), the pub remains a popular site after a decade of operation.

Occupying the ground floor of an office building on West St. Clair Avenue in the city's Warehouse District, the Cleveland Chophouse and Brewery opened in 1998. Owned by Rock Bottom Restaurants, Inc. (who own the nearby Rock Bottom Brewery as well), this is one of three Chophouse restaurants in the United States. Decorated in a 1940s style, with swing and big band music playing, the Chophouse restaurant features a variety of American dishes. The restaurant's 8-barrel brewing system produces around 500 barrels per year.

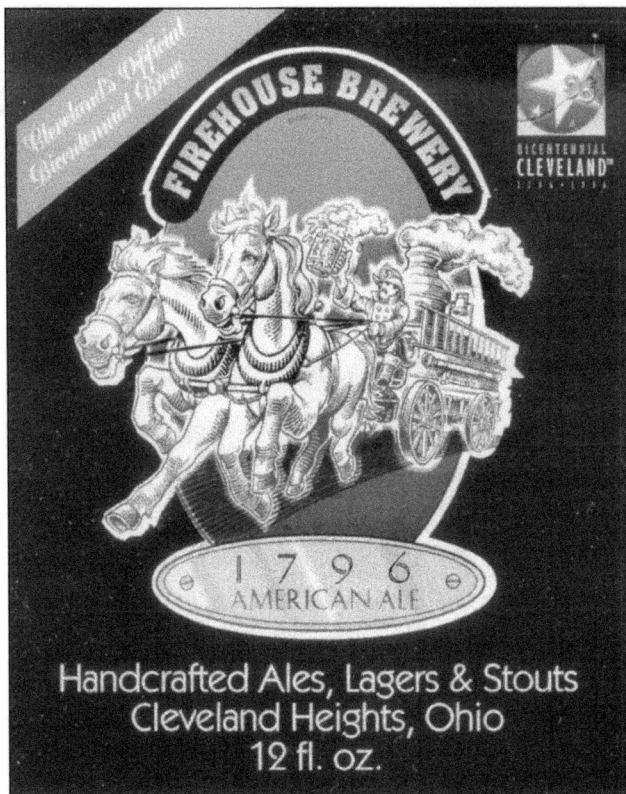

1796 AMERICAN ALE

Handcrafted Ales, Lagers & Stouts
Cleveland Heights, Ohio
12 fl. oz.

Located on Silsby Road in Cleveland Heights, the Firehouse Brewery got its name from its location in a renovated 70-year-old fire station. Opening for business in 1995, the brewpub employed Henryk Orlik as its brewmaster, and his imported European 15-barrel brewing system had an annual capacity of 2,800 barrels. Among the brews offered were Backdraft Stout and 1796 American Ale, which was the official beer of Cleveland's bicentennial celebration in 1996. Although a small bottling line was installed at the site, rapid growth of the brewery took its toll on the company's finances, and by the end of 1997, Firehouse had closed its doors for good.

Cleveland's third microbrewery, the Western Reserve Brewing Company opened in July 1997 in a former armored car warehouse on Commerce Avenue, on the city's east side. Andrew Craze was the head brewer and Gavin Smith was the company's CEO. Their 20-barrel brewing system allowed an annual capacity of 4,500 barrels. Three styles were available year-round: Western Reserve American Wheat Beer, Amber Ale, and Nut Brown Ale. Despite winning numerous awards for its beers, the company continued to accumulate debt with each attempt to expand production and marketing, leaving it forever in the red. By early 2002, it had ceased operations.

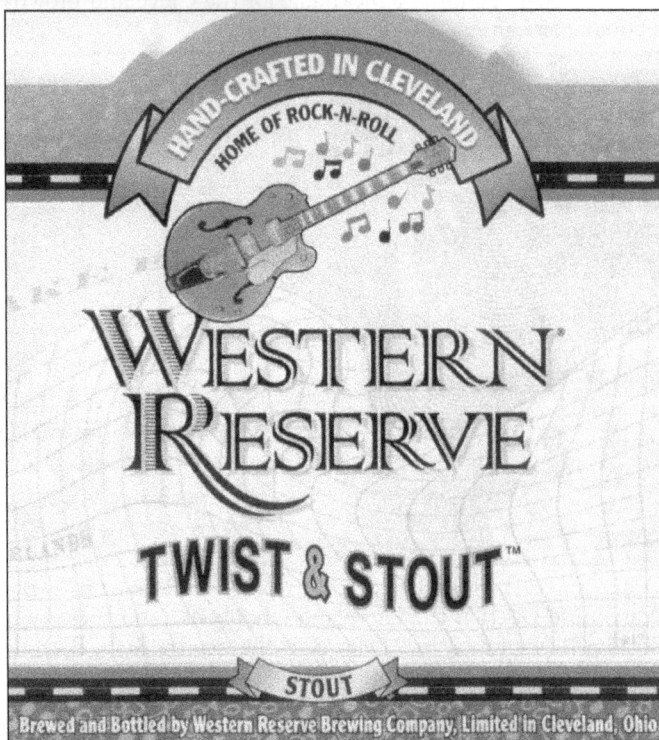

HAND-CRAFTED IN CLEVELAND
HOME OF ROCK-N-ROLL

WESTERN RESERVE

TWIST & STOUT

STOUT

Brewed and Bottled by Western Reserve Brewing Company, Limited in Cleveland, Ohio

The first of three Wallaby's Grille and Brewpub franchises in the region opened in May 1995. Located on Clemens Road in suburban Westlake, adjacent to Interstate 90, all of its beers, food, and décor had an Australian theme. A 10-barrel brewing system was used to produce what became the three standard Wallaby's brands: Great White Wheat Beer, Ayers Rock Pale Ale, and Big Red Roo Strong Ale, with an annual output of approximately 1000 barrels.

The Wallaby's group eventually opened additional brewpubs in downtown Cleveland and in suburban Medina, as well as three non-brewing restaurants as far west as Sandusky. This delivery truck transported barreled beer from the brewery in Westlake to the outlying restaurants, as well as bottled beer to selected stores in the area. By 2000, however, the brewpub trend in the region was in decline, and Wallaby's was among the casualties, with all brewing sites closing.

Serving as the headquarters for the Wallaby's group of brewpubs, the Local Brewing Company opened in 1997 on Sperry Drive in Westlake. The facility brewed and packaged all three of the Wallaby's brands of bottled beer and also performed contract brewing for outside distributors, doing business as the Pilsener Brewing Company. The latter appeared in early 1999, along with its popular old brand, P.O.C. Initial interest and media coverage for the new beer seemed to focus on nostalgia as much as anything, and sales were good that year. However, the brand and distribution company had disappeared without a trace by the end of 2000. The Local Brewing Company itself closed soon after this, along with the entire Wallaby's brewpub group.

One short-lived brewpub was John Harvard's Brewhouse, located on Old River Road in the Flats district in the old Customs House. Part of a nationwide chain of restaurants, John Harvard's opened in 1997 but only lasted until 1999. Later that year, the pub reopened under new ownership and a new brewer as the House of Brews. Success again eluded the restaurant, as it closed for good by the following year.

LIFT BRIDGE BREWING CO.

OKTOBERFEST

BEER

12 FL OZ

The city of Ashtabula lies one hour east of Cleveland, and it was home to its own microbrewery between 1994 and 1998. Costing $200,000 to establish, the Lift Bridge Brewing Company was the brainchild of Dan Madden and Ken Frisbie. The name was a reference to the large bascule-type drawbridge over Ashtabula Harbor, one of only two such bridges in the country. The plant had an annual capacity of 15,000 barrels, and numerous styles of beer were produced in bottles and kegs, which were distributed throughout eastern Ohio and even as far south as Cincinnati, as well as into western Pennsylvania.

Located on Erie Street in downtown Willoughby, the Willoughby Brewing Company had its grand opening in February 1998. The brewery and associated restaurant are situated in a building constructed in 1897 to house the repair shop for the Cleveland, Painesville, and Eastern Railroad Company. Established by owner T. J. Reagan and a group of local investors, the brewing operation consists of a 15-barrel brewhouse, which cost approximately $1.3 million. Among the beers produced is Railway Razz, which has won numerous awards at national beer-tasting events. A limited amount of the beer is kegged and bottled for distribution across a three-county area.

Ohio's first brewed-on-premises facility, the Brew Kettle opened for business in December 1995. Originally located on the south side of suburban Strongsville, it later moved to its current location at 8377 Pearl Road, where it operates in conjunction with a small microbrewery, the Ringneck Brewing Company. Amateur brewers can choose from 60 different recipes to brew batches (just over 12 gallons) of nearly any type of beer, with all the ingredients, equipment, and instruction provided by the staff. After several weeks (depending on the brew), the batch is packaged into six cases of bottles, with customized labels for the customer. Numerous awards have been won by owner and brewer Chris McKim for the brands produced by Ringneck, which are bottled for sale in local establishments.

The Cleveland area's second brewed-on-premises facility, the Brew Keeper, opened in April 1997 at 25200 Miles Road in suburban Bedford Heights. Like the Brew Kettle in Strongsville, the site consists of personal brewing facilities for customers, as well as a small microbrewery, known as the Buckeye Brewing Company. Novice brewers can brew nearly any type of beer, brewing just over 12 gallons at a time in one of the six kettles. The staff provides all the ingredients, recipes, equipment, and instruction. This is also Ohio's first site that allows customers to make a wide variety of their own wines. The microbrewery uses a 3-barrel brewing system, which yields an annual capacity around 300 barrels, much of which is packaged in 22-ounce bottles for sale at area stores. Garin Wright (shown below) has been the brewer of this family-owned establishment since the beginning. (Photograph by Karen Bujak of the *Great Lakes Brewing News*.)

Located on Center Ridge Road, approximately eight miles west of downtown Cleveland in suburban Rocky River, the Rocky River Brewing Company opened as a brewpub in July 1998. Furnished with luxurious oak fixtures and an enormous bar, the brewpub is owned by brothers Bob and Gary Cintron. Utilizing a seven-barrel brewing system (part of which is shown below), brewmaster Matt Cole produces one standard, popular brew: Coopers Gold Kolsch. The remainder of his lineup of beers rotates out of a total of 46 that he chooses from, including several that have won national awards at beer-tasting events. All beer brewed (approximately 600 barrels per year) is sold on site.

One of the area's most unique brewpub settings is that of the Northfield Park Microbrewery, which opened in 1998 at the city's harness racing track. Located on Northfield Road, at the line between Cuyahoga and Summit Counties, the track was built in 1957 on the site of an earlier greyhound track built in 1934 by mobster Al Capone. The brewhouse tanks are located at the park's entrance and can be viewed by all who enter.

GOVERNMENT WARNING: (1) ACCORDING TO THE SURGEON GENERAL, WOMEN SHOULD NOT DRINK ALCOHOLIC BEVERAGES DURING PREGNANCY BECAUSE OF THE RISK OF BIRTH DEFECTS. (2) CONSUMPTION OF ALCOHOLIC BEVERAGES IMPAIRS YOUR ABILITY TO DRIVE A CAR OR OPERATE MACHINERY, AND MAY CAUSE HEALTH PROBLEMS.

Best if enjoyed before

A thick and satisfying chocolate-colored beer with a rich, full body and deep-roasted malt flavors.

NORTHFIELD PARK

9

40-1 STOUT

RACETRACK & BREWERY

12 FL OZ (355 ML)

40-1 STOUT
Win big. Play the long shot! Deep-roasted barley and oats give this "meal in a bottle" a rich and robust malt flavor. 40-1 Stout will definitely stick to your ribs with its bold body and linger on your palate with its smooth and satisfying taste. A thick, frothy head crowns this dark beer.

40-1 Stout is one of the many fine lagers, ales and soft drinks handcrafted by our master brewer. Using the freshest ingredients available in original recipes, Northfield Park brews are sure to stimulate the palates of craft brewing fans everywhere.

Ingredients: Water, malted barley, oats, hops, yeast.

Brewed & bottled by:
Northfield Park Micro-Brewery
Northfield, Ohio 44067

David Gunn is the brewer for the Northfield Park Microbrewery, and among the numerous beer styles that he makes are Crimson Colt Ale, Silks Cream Ale, Winners Wheat, and 40-1 Stout. A small amount of these brands is bottled with labels like this one, for sale at the racetrack's dining room.

One of the area's newest offerings is the Quarryman Taverne and Church Street Brewery, which opened in 2001 in suburban Berea. Operated by brewer Dave Sutula and, later, Doug Beedy, the brewpub had a quaint setting just two blocks from Baldwin-Wallace College. Although it closed in 2003, the pub reopened with new ownership in late 2004 under the name Cornerstone Brewing Company, which continues to operate today.

While the overall number of brewpubs and microbreweries has dwindled from its peak in the late 1990s, many Ohioans, and Clevelanders in particular, still enjoy craft-brewed beers. More brewpubs are due to open in the region in the near future, and Great Lakes is poised to be around for the long haul. The brewing of beer in the Cleveland area is likely to continue for many years.

www.ingramcontent.com/pod-product-compliance
Lightning Source LLC
Chambersburg PA
CBHW080602110426
42813CB00006B/1383